A YEAR AND SOME CHANGE

Revealing Your Full Potential through Purpose and Perspective

REGINALD BEAN

G Corvin
Thank you for the
inspiration

Ideas In Motion, LLC
Waxhaw, North Carolina

A Year and Some Change
Revealing Your Full Potential through Purpose and Perspective
Reginald Bean

Published by Ideas in Motion, LLC, Charlotte, NC.

Designed and produced by SPARK Publications, SPARKpublications.com, Charlotte, NC.

Printed in the United States of America.
Paperback, June 2018, ISBN: 978-0-692-09371-9
E-book, June 2018, ISBN: 978-0-692-13430-6
Library of Congress Control Number: 2018945276

SEL027000   **SELF-HELP** / Personal Growth / Success
SEL023000   **SELF-HELP** / Personal Growth / Self-Esteem
FAM000000   **FAMILY & RELATIONSHIPS** / General

DEDICATION

This book is dedicated to the emerging generation of leaders who have decided to inspire the world, to live authentically, and to impact, influence, and embrace change.

This book is also dedicated to the people who've helped shape me into the person I am today. Thank you to my friends, family, business and spiritual leaders, mentors, and the many men (young and seasoned) who have encouraged me by allowing me to share life's journey with them.

Table of Contents

RANDOM THOUGHTS

This space is for you to capture random thoughts as you progress through this book.

_____

_____

_____

_____

_____

_____

_____

_____

_____

_____

_____

_____

_____

_____

_____

_____

_____

Introduction

"We all feel helpless and frustrated by the violence. We do. But that's not acceptable. It's time to look in the mirror and ask ourselves, 'What are we doing to create change?' It's not about being a role model. It's not about our responsibility to the tradition of activism. I know tonight we're honoring Muhammad Ali—the GOAT. But to do his legacy any justice, let's use this moment as a call to action for all professional athletes to educate ourselves. It's for these issues. Speak up. Use our influence. And renounce all violence. And most importantly, go back to our communities, invest our time, our resources, help rebuild them, help strengthen them, help change them. We all have to do better. Thank you."

I watched in awe as LeBron James delivered this bold challenge to a decorated, star-studded 2016 ESPY Awards audience (Chan 2016). It was a necessary call to action for athletes to become the change they want to see in the world. While many of us may look at athletes and assign more responsibility as change agents, in this case I immediately looked at myself and asked, "What are you doing to create change?"

Are you a change agent? Or do you complain about "them" and all the things "they" are doing to "us"? In this country, we are fortunate to have the freedom of choice. We can choose to accept our current situation or take the necessary steps to improve it. Now, I realize that sometimes the choice isn't as simple as it sounds; however, I'm referring to the things that we actually control.

I remember my grandmother was great about telling us that we could be whatever we wanted in life. Regardless of the dream, if we wanted to be mayor, she would say go for it. If we wanted to be a teacher, she would say go for it. Many kids are told from a young age, "You can be anything you want to be; the possibilities are endless." Hearing that gives us great confidence, just like my grandmother telling her grandkids. But what about kids who aren't told that? Or kids like me, who might be told about the endless possibilities and walk out into the world with a different reality? Walking out of my home in Detroit was pretty symbolic of this experience. It was nice and safe and warm inside, but stepping out into the cold brought a new reality. Similarly, any sense of hope that was instilled immediately vanished. The reality of hopelessness, violence, and dysfunction was evident walking through a neighborhood where homes had bars on the windows to prevent unwanted guests and guys hanging out on the streets without any real sense of purpose in life.

Looking back on my life now, I can see that the words of encouragement were nothing more than setting the expectations for my life. Those words of encouragement simply planted seeds of accountability, ownership, and the idea that I was responsible for the parts of my life that I could control. The question that I had to answer, even at a young age, was why was I doing the things that I was doing, dreaming the dreams that I was dreaming, or better yet, behaving the way that I was (either positively or negatively). The truth is, I was influenced by the expectations of those around me and the media, including statistics that reminded me and others born in zip codes similar to mine that we would either be dead, in jail, or incapable of contributing to society as adults, rather than being successful at our jobs, dedicated husbands, or highly involved fathers.

MY EVOLUTION BEGAN WITH OWNING THREE AREAS OF MY LIFE: MY MIND, MY LOCATION, AND MY CIRCLE.

One lesson that I learned early in life is that we're not shaped by others' expectations, and we aren't limited by the expectations others place on us. In fact, we are in control of our own lives.

Since then, I have realized there is more to that equation. It's not enough to point out the possibilities. We have to provide a set of instructions to show people how to grab them, how to take control of their lives.

Let me tell you, this mentality is real. People are actually living up to (or down to) the expectations of others. This pattern has been studied by researchers, including Rosenthal, Jacobsen, and Babad, who labeled it the Pygmalion effect. "When we expect certain behaviors of others, we are likely to act in ways that make the expected behavior more likely to occur" (Rosenthal and Babad 1985). Explained loosely, this means that we are living our lives based on what other people expect out of us, whether positive or negative.

My evolution began with owning three areas of my life that I could control: my mind, my location, and my circle. **Changing my mind** (how I see myself and the possibilities in life) involved rearranging my internal thoughts and perceived barriers that caused self-esteem and insecurity limitations. **Changing my location** (moving out of a dysfunctional environment and/or toward opportunities) was the realization that my dreams, ambition, and purpose resided outside of my current environment and that I had to find a vehicle to get closer to the opportunity. Lastly, **Changing my circle** (choosing a different set of friends and role models, and distancing myself from certain people) was about surrounding myself with different people, people who thought differently or had achieved the level of success that I saw in myself.

The thing is, each one of us has the power to change our outcomes. The only one holding us back is the person we each see in the mirror. We have control over our own lives. Rather than letting other people's expectations control your life, take control of your own expectations. We have the power to change our outcomes and shape where our futures lead.

One of my goals is to change how people view change—to change how we view expectations of ourselves. The power to shape who we are—to change our outcomes—comes from within. It's not dependent on our friends, our teachers, our bosses, or even our families. It's all within us. We have the tools to make the change. We have the power. The goal is to learn how to access that power and change our futures, to make our lives go in the directions we want them to go.

I want to encourage you to let go of other people's expectations and really take the time to figure out who you are and where you want to go and to channel that power to make things happen.

That's what brings me to this book, *A Year and Some Change.* I challenge you to take the next year and a few additional months to look at yourself, explore what you expect from yourself and from life, and answer the question, "What great impact will I have on my community and family?" Through the process of this book, we will work on setting realistic goals and then focus on how to change your expectations and set a clear path for your future while providing the tools you need to get there. We all have something to contribute, and we all have within us the potential to be anything we want to be. It's just a matter of finding the power within yourself to make a change, to get your life on the right track.

A Year and Some Change is designed to issue the same challenge for each of us to not sit by and wish for someone else to solve the concerns in our schools or social issues in our communities. I want this book to encourage each of us to pick one area of our lives, communities, or social circles to change. With the amount of discourse going on in society today, it's easy to expect someone else to solve the problem. I would like to hit the point that change begins with each of us taking responsibility for our own actions, and that will lead to change in our communities and ultimately change within the world. But you, the reader, has to choose the area you would like to change and then work to make it happen.

WE ALL HAVE THE TOOLS INSIDE US TO IMPACT CHANGE.

After the Ball Drops:
New Beginnings

Cultures around the world have New Year's Eve traditions designed to bring good luck or good fortune into the home and to symbolize starting a New Year with a clean slate. Some traditions include eating certain foods to bring good luck. Others include cleaning the entire house to start the year out on the right foot.

In England, the custom for welcoming the New Year is full of hospitality and warmth. They believe the first guest for the year will bring good luck throughout the year. In China, they have a unique way of celebrating New Year—the front door of every house is painted red, a color that symbolizes happiness and good fortune. They also hide all the knives for the day so that no one cuts oneself because that may actually cut the entire family's good luck for the coming year. Finally, Brazilians believe that lentils signify wealth and prosperity, so they serve foods like soup or rice made with legumes for the New Year's meal. Each culture might have something very different that they do, but the point of all the traditions is about preparing their immediate environment for what could be in the coming year and the possibility of a change for the better.

In addition to special foods, cleaning house, and hiding knives, many of us also make New Year's resolutions. That tradition might stem in part from the endless possibilities available in a New Year. Most of us are looking at January 1 as a fresh start, a clean slate, which makes it a perfect time to try something new or set new goals. Some of the most popular resolutions are things like kicking a smoking habit, losing weight, exercising more, or getting out of toxic relationships.

While these are all great aspirations, one amazing point is, generally speaking, we don't have to wait until New Year's Eve to make a decision to change our lives for the better. In fact, there's really nothing special about making a resolution on New Year's Day.

ONE OUT OF THREE OF THOSE PEOPLE HAVE GIVEN UP ON THEIR GOALS BY THE END OF JANUARY.

Although our resolutions are meant to kick the year off with a new perspective, one research firm, Harris Interactive, reminds us that somewhere around 45 percent of Americans make New Year's resolutions, while one out of three of those people have given up on their goals by the end of January.

We start out with great intentions and have admirable goals. So why is it that many of us fail to follow through with our New Year's resolutions? Consider this: we often adapt vague goals without clear guidelines or specific plans. Rather than focusing on changing people, places, or problems, we aim for something big and all-encompassing but don't take the steps necessary to follow through. Many of our resolutions avoid focusing on the one thing or, better yet, area that could redirect the future of our lives or our minds.

A good resolution will work on changing your perspectives regarding yourself instead of changing something outside yourself. Simply put, making the verbal commitment to change is a great first step, but just because we wish for something to happen doesn't necessarily mean that it will happen. Many things can cause our well-intentioned resolutions to derail—anything from not having the right tools in place, the right support systems around us, or ultimately not focusing on ourselves and changing how we think. Without the right tools, support, and mindset, we're basically ensuring we don't meet our goals at the end of the year successfully.

In one of my favorite books, *The Power of Habit: Why We Do What We Do in Life and Business*, author Charles Duhigg states, "If you believe you can change—if you make it a habit—the change becomes real" (2012). That is the real meaning of making a resolution and sticking with it: believing that you can change and that the power to change is in yourself. And when you make it a habit, the change becomes real.

Things became real for me one day during my senior year of high school. My friend Lawrence and I were sitting in his mom's basement after working a shift at a famous fried-chicken restaurant. This day wasn't much different than any other day, except it was. Instead of simply passing time talking about sports or the latest cute girl to come through our line at work, we sat restless. Sitting there with the smell of fried chicken heavy in the air, we were dreaming about how our lives would be so different in just a few weeks. Granted, our work ethic in the classroom didn't match our ambition outside the classroom; however, both of us had acceptance letters to college, and we were looking forward to a change of scenery.

"Man, I can't wait to get out of this place," I said.

"I know. No more standing over fryers for hours for a few bucks. We'll be taking college classes, living in the dorm, living the dream," Lawrence said.

And that's when it hit us. Exactly whose dream would we be living?

"You know, even when we're at college, we'll still have to come back to the same environment," I said.

"I guess you're right," Lawrence answered. "And we'll still have to come back here during breaks."

"Man, even when we go to college, we're still stuck here," I said.

"Yeah, and here isn't where we want to be," Lawrence said.

That's when it hit me—my epiphany! The key to a better life. We needed to change our location, to put ourselves in an entirely new situation. Otherwise, we risked the same path as the kids who had graduated from high school a few years before us who I now saw working jobs without the promise of a productive life. These were smart, ambitious kids who could have had bright futures. But they fell victim to the expectations of our neighborhood and society. It looked like we were predestined to a future that didn't look too different than the one we'd experienced to that point.

For Lawrence and me, the thought of college and the change it would bring wasn't good enough. We wanted real change. It was something we had talked about for years, but how were we going to get it? We knew that in order to have a chance to fulfill all the dreams we had talked about, we needed to change our location. In this case, a radical change was necessary—much more than going to college. We decided to join the Army. That day in the basement, he and I both decided to give up our college acceptances and join the military. Neither of us had a patriotic sense to serve and fight for our country; it was really just a way out of our neighborhood, where boys grew up to be men who weren't around for their families and children, who lived lives of crime, or who never even made it to adulthood. We felt like we'd finally figured out how we were going to change our lives forever.

Here's the deal—Lawrence and I had been friends since the sixth grade. We connected almost immediately, both being somewhat of the outsiders in the class. My classmates liked me well enough, but we didn't really hang out. They were getting into things that weren't attractive to me, things that I would say were normal for many urban, inner-city kids. Lawrence, as a new kid to the middle school, was also an outsider. So it was an instant bond.

It might have seemed a little strange to others since we were very much opposites. I was a pretty quiet and tolerant kid, not wanting to stir up much trouble. I guess some would say I saw the best in people or avoided what I knew could be dangerous, contentious situations. Lawrence, on the other hand, was outgoing but somewhat of a hot head. He might get the party going or a fight started; it simply depended on the situation. We were like yin and yang together, and it was our shared ambition that formed our bond.

Lawrence and I both applied and were accepted to the same college. After all of our talk of doing something better with our lives, of breaking the patterns we saw around us of dysfunctional families and unfulfilled dreams, we felt like we finally found a way.

But that day, with our college acceptance letters in one hand and our weekly checks in the other, we started to realize something. College wasn't the ticket out we thought it was. The total change in location was.

Leaving for the Army was just like making a New Year's resolution. I was going to join the Army in order to change my circumstance, and it sounded like a great idea at the time. But in reality, it was similar to someone who decides to quit smoking or lose weight. It's a goal but one that doesn't address the root cause of the issue.

I knew I wanted real change, and joining the Army represented that for me. But once I made that decision, I still had hurdles in my way.

I knew I wanted to change. And I was using the tools available to me to make that change. For me, that meant having Lawrence there at my side as an accountability partner, encouraging me along the way, even as he was going through the same process. It meant convincing my mom and others in my family that just because I was doing something different, it wasn't necessarily wrong. After all, I wanted to find a way to do something different with my life.

Here's what I realized through that experience: we all have the tools inside us to impact change—the power to change who we are and to get to wherever "there" is because that power comes from within, not from other people's expectations of who we are or who we should be. The point of many New Year's resolutions is to change our lives for the better, but in order to make it happen we need to change who we are on the inside.

I didn't make my decision to change on New Year's Eve, but I feel that comparing my decision to a New Year's resolution is important. That excited, euphoric feeling of realizing the need to do something different—you know, the sense of hope we all feel at the beginning of the year—is an important driver in helping us change our own lives. It is the motivation that helps us take the first step to changing our circumstances or situations, to be the best person we each can be.

Here's my message to you: the first step in making a change in our lives is realizing the need for change and making that a goal. I'm not referring to the superficial, where you post to social media, so everyone can see you want to change. I'm referring to the type of change that can impact your entire family, community, or school; change that comes not only in the form of making goals or resolutions but also in learning to take control of your own life; the type of change that will force you to let go of other people's expectations and take control of where your life is going. Once you are in the driver's seat of life, firmly take control of the wheel, and own the path that you're on and the direction of your life, you are more likely to stay on the right path rather than veering off.

THE FIRST STEP IN MAKING A CHANGE IN OUR LIVES IS REALIZING THE NEED FOR CHANGE AND MAKING THAT A GOAL.

Over the course of this year, you will walk through the steps necessary to make that change in your own life. Our objective is to begin with setting goals. These will be realistic and specific goals. The way to do this is to focus on one area of your life, one area that can have a significant impact on your journey. Once you've decided to change, realize that decision is only the first step in a long process.

Once you've decided that enough is enough and to make a change, it's time to take inventory of your life. Will you need to change your mind, change your location, or change your circle? It might be one; it might be all three.

Look around you. Are you blaming your friends or family for your circumstances? Are you owning your decisions in life? I'm not proposing you alienate yourself from your family. It's more a matter of talking things over with them, making it clear to them what you want out of life, and even asking for their support if they're willing to get on board.

The thing is, change can begin with a resolution or a goal. But that is only the beginning. True change—I mean the change that can impact your family for generations to come—will require you to look in the mirror and begin with yourself. Real change will force you to evaluate whose expectations and dreams you are attempting to live up (or down) to. For Lawrence and me, it was acceptable for us to apply and go to college. Those were expectations in our neighborhood, but the expectation was also there that we would come back. And Lawrence and I were aware that coming back meant falling into the trap of other people's expectations for our futures, expectations that weren't what we wanted. Our change meant making a permanent change in location. That was me. Yours will be different. But what is the same is that you have to realize the change within yourself. Are you internalizing the expectations of society, media, social media, family, or friends? Be aware of the sources that you are receiving input from in your life.

I made the decision to change my life by first changing my

mind and my desire for a more fulfilling and purposeful life. Then I changed my location. I joined the military to make that change, and it led me on a whole new path. Your change might be different. It might mean going to college when no one in your family has before. It might mean deciding to break up with a boyfriend or girlfriend. The important thing to remember is that change can be good, the power to change comes from within, and we all have the power to make the change.

start small

Set goals that you're more likely to stick with. It's easier to stay on track with a realistic, specific goal. Plus, you're less likely to get discouraged and quit altogether.

outline your plan

Decide how you will deal with the temptation to skip that exercise class or have that piece of cake. This could include calling on a friend for help or reminding yourself how missing will affect your goal.

track your progress

Keep track of each small success. Short-term goals are easier to keep, and each small accomplishment will help keep you motivated. Keep a journal to help you stay on track and reward yourself for each five pounds lost.

Write down *one* change that you would like to make this year.

_____

_____

_____

_____

_____

Certain distractions could prevent me from working toward my change. Here's how I plan to counteract them.

Barriers & Distractions	Counteraction

DREAMING CREATES A VISION; LEARNING SOMETHING NEW IS WHAT MAKES IT ALL HAPPEN.

CHAPTER 2

Become More Active:
The Dreamer

Some would say that a New Year's resolution is about a rebirth—you know, an opportunity to be thoughtful and mindful about where you are and who you'd like to be. For many, a focus on health seems like a logical place to scrutinize, following the carbohydrate binge during Thanksgiving and Christmas. Some people don't really have a weight problem, and they even get some exercise a few times a week. Still, most of their days consist of sitting around most of the time at home and at work, which can have a potential negative effect on their health.

If you don't fall into the previous category—perhaps you're overweight with an inactive lifestyle, or you're a beginner in the fitness and activity world who has little or no idea about the pleasures and pains of a healthy, active lifestyle, but you've committed to the goal of changing your lifestyle and increasing your activities—you may feel that it's time to get off your behind and improve your mental and physical state. So you adopt some healthy and active New Year's resolution tips to enjoy a healthier you. Some tips may include eating more fruits and vegetables, joining a gym, cutting down on certain food groups, trying a new sports activity, broadening your knowledge, or simply spending time with friends and family to increase your activity level.

Many experts would suggest that resolutions, ambitions, and goals should include concrete plans with specific goals. But dreaming about a different life is part of the process. Embracing a new, active lifestyle can be more than just physical activities and can include mental activities such as visualizing and dreaming about the future.

DREAMING ABOUT A DIFFERENT LIFE IS PART OF THE PROCESS.

I remember how I used to dream.

I couldn't believe where I was sitting. Rubbing my hands on the leather seats of a bright red Corvette with the T-tops out, I was mesmerized by that dashboard. In Detroit, cars are a way of life and meant everything as the lifeblood of the city. But I had never been in a car like this, with all the bells and whistles. I turned the key in the ignition and felt the power of that car. I was sitting there thinking, "I'm only sixteen years old, and I'm sitting here in a Corvette. This car costs more than my mom's house." That was just the start.

I started daydreaming—about driving that car, about what kind of man it was who actually owned the car, what he did to get a car like that, what type of life he led, what his family looked like, what his house looked like—"Hey, man, that guy's waiting."

I was rudely awakened from my daydream by another runner. I guess I had gotten so caught up in my daydreams, sitting there in that Corvette, that I forgot where I was and what I was supposed to be doing. I was working as a valet parker, and the actual owner of the car was waiting for me to bring it to him.

I signed up for the cash but ended up getting a lot more than that from the experience. That job took me out of our neighborhood and exposed me to something different. It took me to the suburbs, really just a few miles away from my inner-city Detroit neighborhood, but it felt like a different world. We were parking cars for people at bar mitzvahs, weddings, retirement parties, and whatever other events needed this type of service.

The job itself was relatively easy, and I can say it was a lot of fun to be in the driver's seat of everything from soccer-mom minivans to expensive sports cars, even for just a few minutes. But the job ended up being so much more than just a way to earn a little extra money. It was truly an eye-opening experience. For the first time in my life, I was exposed to something different. The food was different. Conversation topics were foreign. People seemed happy. Where I came from, when that many people got together, you almost always had a good time, but there was a difference. This was often festive, joyous.

And what made an even bigger impact on me were the large families. We'd be working a bar mitzvah where the kid would have both his parents there along with grandparents and sometimes even a great-grandparent. Generations all came together, celebrating one kid.

As soon as that other runner came knocking on the window of that red Corvette, I drove the car back to its owner. I didn't want to do anything to jeopardize that opportunity. But the few minutes I sat there had a lasting impression. I started thinking about what my life could be like if I got out of where I was. Seeing a different side of life, in the suburbs of Detroit, was one step in helping me realize I wanted more out of life.

There were other things in my life that helped expose me to a life different than what I was living in my own neighborhood. I was lucky to have a particular man in my life, Darryl Ounanian, a youth pastor who really dedicated his life to changing expectations for the kids in my neighborhood. He opened up the church basement every Friday night for movie nights with free pizza, and we all thought we were getting a great deal, pizza and a movie. What we were really getting was a way to stay safe and off the streets. He also took us on trips, and it was through the ski trip to Wisconsin that I experienced something new, another thing that helped build on my dream to change the outcome of my life.

When Sir Nose, as we called him, took me and a bunch of kids from my neighborhood skiing, it was the first time most of us had been to the ski slopes. None of us had the bibs or equipment, but it didn't stop us from having fun. I looked around and saw something was different. I maybe didn't understand it completely at the time, but I saw it. Here, in a different environment, people were different. The new experience was impactful and something I knew I wanted to continue.

All of these experiences helped create a dream within me. It wasn't the actual skiing or the big houses and fancy cars that I wanted. I wanted the opportunities, the chance to make my life different. It was then I began to have a dream for something different in my life. It was the dream that sparked my change and started me on a journey that totally changed my life. But the important thing is, it all started with a dream.

The decision to change came from within, but before I made any decisions I had to visualize it, dream about it. Dreaming is what begins the process. I began by imagining myself out of a situation; then my actions followed my thoughts.

My dream of getting out of my neighborhood helped make the things around me—the violence, the dysfunction, the crime—matter less. That stuff didn't impact me as much anymore because I knew I wanted something different. I wasn't going to become that. I was going to be different.

My dream took shape gradually. It started with my grandmother telling me I could be anything I wanted in life. She helped me realize I could be more than what I saw in the neighborhood. Then through experiences like working as a valet, I saw there was a different life out there than what I was living. I saw it, but I didn't know how to get there. Being exposed to different environments and learning something new helped me realize that I didn't have to live up to the explicit or implied expectations set out by my environment.

MY DREAM OF GETTING OUT OF MY NEIGHBORHOOD HELPED MAKE THE THINGS AROUND ME—THE VIOLENCE, THE DYSFUNCTION, THE CRIME—MATTER LESS.

Realizing there was more to life, visualizing my future in a different way was one thing that helped reinforce my dream.

What type of change are you looking for this year? More specifically, why is change important in your life? Are you changing expectations of your future, changing where you are in life, changing how you view your life? It's all a part of evolving into the person you want to be. And it all starts with a dream. Dreaming creates a vision; learning something new is what makes it all happen.

Everyone's dream is different and learning style unique. But the way to finding your dream is the same. Ask yourself, do you want something different from your life? Do you see yourself making an impact? Start to imagine what you want, what your future looks like. And then write it down. Once you've written down your vision, it's much easier to develop it into something more than just a dream.

Whether you have a dream of becoming an athlete, a chef, or a business professional, it's important to know your dream is valid. It's not just a pie-in-the-sky aspiration. Writing it down helps it become more real. It also helps you gain focus.

Once you write out your dream share it with someone that you trust. Having an accountability partner to help you keep on track can help keep your dream alive. It's important to have someone to have your back and keep you dreaming, even when times get tough.

dream big

Audacious goals are compelling. Want to compete in a marathon or triathlon? With perseverance, encouragement, and support, you can do it.

don't overcomplicate the process

Sometimes we think dreaming is silly or something harder than it really has to be, and we put it off visualizing something different for our lives.

make dreaming a part of your everyday

It's important not to see dreaming as a one-time event. Sometimes we tend to see learning as something separate from our everyday lives, but it really isn't.

WHAT DOES THE VISION IN YOUR DREAM LOOK LIKE?

Draw it.

This month's goal targets are:

_____

_____

_____

_____

Today I'm grateful for these three things:

1 _____
_____
_____

2 _____
_____
_____

3 _____
_____
_____

ORGANIZING OUR THOUGHTS INTO A PLAN CAN BE THE FIRST STEP IN CREATING CHANGE IN OUR LIVES.

Get Organized:
The Master Plan

You probably don't belong on an episode of *Hoarders*, but there's a good chance your life could use a little more organization. On just about every New Year's resolution top ten list, getting organized is near the top and can be a very reasonable goal. With the New Year as motivation, getting started right away is a good idea. Whether you want your car organized enough that you can give someone a ride on a whim, or your bedroom organized enough that you can find the remote control when you need it, this chapter should get you started on the way to a more organized life.

Before you dive right into donating your outdated shoe collection, ask yourself, what is the purpose of the resolution? How will my life improve once I achieve the goal? At the outset, adjust your vision for organization from a monumental task to zero in on one or two specific, actionable areas. Also, if you try to do too much at once, it's easy to become overwhelmed and frustrated. Instead, start with small steps and develop consistency and small wins. Pace yourself; this way you'll feel a sense of accomplishment and the motivation to do more. Here's an example of organizing my thoughts into a game plan for life, which may help you achieve a decidedly organized New Year.

Who would have thought that a five-minute stop for gas would change the direction of my life? Flashing emergency vehicle lights at 2 a.m. is never a welcoming sight. This particular night, my friend whom I was riding with had to stop to get gas. He had borrowed his mom's car and didn't want to return it to her empty. This was a typical summer night in Detroit, hanging out on the downtown scene along the riverfront, six of us divided into two cars. The other guys we had been hanging out with were in two other cars and drove on home. We followed behind them about ten minutes later.

As we approached the flashing lights, my heart started to beat a little faster. Then we got closer and saw it wasn't just the blue lights of the police. There were the red lights of an ambulance, and fire trucks were on the scene as well. It was chaos, and we weren't close enough yet to see what exactly was going on. I was starting to get worried.

We couldn't drive all the way up to my house, so we parked the car and started down towards the scene. As we got closer, I recognized the car right in the middle of all the activity. It belonged to one of the friends we'd been with that night. And seconds later, I looked over and saw my friend lying there on the stretcher, EMTs working to stop the bleeding and get him stabilized from a gunshot wound.

The situation wasn't fatal. But he was badly hurt and would suffer consequences of that night for the rest of his life. I found out later that as he was driving up to drop off our other friend who was riding with him, a car drove by openly shooting. My friend who had been shot had been involved in an incident with another guy a few days earlier, but he thought the situation was over. The violence that night showed us all it wasn't over. But more than anything, it showed me how fast life can take a turn.

I stood there, watching my friend fight for his life on that stretcher, and all I could think was, "That could have been me." Sure, I wasn't in the middle of many confrontations. But that shooting showed me all those things didn't matter. My life could have been altered just because of the place I lived. If we hadn't stopped for gas, it could have just as easily been me on that stretcher. We would have all arrived at the same time, and the guys shooting from the car weren't random shooters. They were shooting as much as they could with the intent to do harm.

That incident was different from others that I'd experienced. It lit a fire under me and forced me to evaluate my path. I had known for years I wanted a different life for myself than what I saw around me. I wanted to be successful at something, have a family, be a good dad, but most importantly, live a productive and impactful life. But I realized that night it was going to take changing my environment for me to make sure that all happened.

It was time for me to organize my life and thoughts by creating my master plan.

Up until that point, I had loose, undefined goals. I only knew I wanted something different. But I didn't have a clear idea of how I was going to make it happen. When I saw my friend lying on that stretcher, it became clear what I needed to do, and that was to get out. Getting out of the city and beginning a new chapter in a new location became the first step in my master plan.

As you can see, I didn't have it clearly mapped out. I couldn't predict every detail of my life and where it would lead. But I had goals I wanted to accomplish, and now I had a master plan to shape how I would accomplish those goals.

Organizing our thoughts into a plan can be the first step in creating change in our lives. Creating a plan will also allow us to define the direction of our lives. Remember Dr. Rosenthal's research discovery, the Pygmalion Effect, and the benefit of positive expectations? This was an example in my life where my expectations didn't match the expectations of the environment that I lived in.

IF YOU WANT TO CHANGE THE ENVIRONMENT, YOU HAVE TO COME UP WITH A PLAN FOR YOUR LIFE.

In this book, we've talked about how we have within ourselves the power to change—to change where we are and who we become. The power to change is not only inside us but also totally up to each of us.

If you're reading this book, most likely you've already realized that you need to change something in your life. Whatever change you want in your life, it is up to you to make it happen. It all starts with understanding what you want out of life and then making a plan to make it happen. It could be joining the military, or it could be working hard in the gym or classroom in order to make it to college.

The point is, regardless of our situations (the environments we were been born into), we have the ability to change the outcomes. But hoping and wishing won't make it happen. If you want to change the environment, you have to come up with a plan for your life. Define what you want out of life; that's how you organize your current situation and design your master plan. Then once you have that, figure out what it will take to get there. You might not be able to map out the whole journey, but as long as you know your first step, you are on your way to change. Then finally, start gathering the information and tools you need as you begin changing the outcome of your life.

Having a master plan doesn't mean mapping out every detail. But you do have to have some concrete tasks planned out in order to reach your ultimate goals, and that's what a master plan will do for you. Here are a few tips as you begin to organize your thoughts into a master plan.

change your attitude

Ask yourself, what is the positive result of the resolution? Identify an area of your life that will have a significant impact before getting started.

be realistic

Don't try to "eat the elephant in one bite." Set smaller, more attainable, and specific goals over time rather than one gigantic goal.

stay accountable

Making an agreement with oneself is much easier to fudge. Find someone or a group with whom to commit to organizing your master plan.

Master Plan
Flow Chart

Where You Are Now:

_____

_____

STEP

1

What information or skills do you need to start toward your ultimate goal? Figuring that out is Step 1. Don't worry about the other steps for now. Step 1 is your new goal. And it will help you determine Step 2 and onward.

_____

_____

_____

_____

The journey toward your end goal may not be a straight line. That's normal. Take one step at a time and keep moving. You'll get there.

Your Goal / Where You Want to Be:

_____

_____

RESOLVING TO LEARN SOMETHING NEW CAN BE EXCITING, AND THE WORLD IS FULL OF FUN FACTS AND NEW EXPERIENCES.

Learn Something New:
Know Your Why

Have you vowed to make this year the year to learn something new? Perhaps you are considering learning how to code, or do you want to learn a new language or just how to fix your bike? Whether you listen to a podcast or read a book, you'll find learning something new to be one of the easiest, most motivating resolutions to keep. You've been meaning to learn Mandarin. You'd love to play the electric guitar. How great would it be to really know how to cook? Resolving to learn something new can be exciting, and the world is full of fun facts and new experiences. And the process of discovering them, not just the end result, is enjoyable and fulfilling.

Why do you think people make this resolution? In my opinion, as people grow we realize we have to challenge and keep challenging ourselves. In addition to learning, dreaming is an important part of the equation. There's a quote by Anthon St. Maarten that says, "Dare to dream! If you did not have the capability to make your wildest wishes come true, your mind would not have the capacity to conjure such ideas in the first place. There is no limitation on what you can potentially achieve, except for the limitation you choose to impose on your own imagination. What you believe to be possible will always come to pass—to the extent that you deem it possible. It really is as simple as that" (Goodreads n.d.). I recall one of my most vivid dreams along the journey, and I'd like to share.

> **THERE IS NO LIMITATION ON WHAT YOU CAN POTENTIALLY ACHIEVE, EXCEPT FOR THE LIMITATION YOU CHOOSE TO IMPOSE ON YOUR OWN IMAGINATION.**

Several years ago, I found myself in a place where I never thought I would be. I was sitting in a chair in a career counselor's office, filling out paperwork to let them know my skills and interests. This was after starting a new job, only to be laid off after three months when the company restructured. I was out of work, recently divorced, and wondering what had happened in my life. Up until that point, I thought I had everything seemingly under control. From the time I had decided to live a productive life, things had gone pretty well. I got out of the city, served in the military, went to college, got a pretty good job, bought a house, got married—I was checking things off on my list of accomplishments. And then, all of a sudden, it seemed like all the things I thought were important had fallen apart.

I went to the career counselor because it was offered in the severance package, but I didn't have a lot of confidence in the process. I was looking for a job on my own as well, something I had plenty of experience with already.

At my first meeting with the career counselor, he asked, "What can I help you with?" I thought to myself, "What does he mean? He knows why I'm here; he's supposed to help me find my next job." I ignored his question, thinking it was rhetorical, while we looked over the paperwork.

The next week I was back in his office, and he asked that same question: "What can I help you with?" Again, I hesitated. He knew why I was there. Attempting to answer what I thought was a crazy question, I started talking about my interests and goals, some things beyond the typical skill-set questions that career counselors typically ask.

The third visit started the same way: "What can I help you with?" We talked for a while, and then he asked if I had ever thought of volunteering. The local high school was setting up a program to match mentors in the community with young men without male figures in their lives. I told him to go ahead and set me up. Other than looking for work, I had some time on my hands. I might as well do something productive, and mentoring sounded interesting.

The first day I walked into the library of the high school to a group of about twenty fifteen- and sixteen-year-old young men. It was definitely an awkward situation. I wasn't exactly sure what to even talk about, and they were staring at me, probably wondering why they had even signed up for the program in the first place.

When I went into that room the first time, I thought I was coming in to tell these young men how to live their lives—to tell them what they were doing wrong and show them how to turn it around. I found myself trying to force a conversation. But I quickly realized they didn't need someone to tell them what to do. What they needed was someone to talk to, to have a conversation with. They needed to connect with someone, man to man.

The second time I went in, I started out with, "Hey, did you see that football game last night?" And the conversation snowballed from there. I knew I had something to share, but it wasn't what I thought it was at first. What I could share with those guys was my own experience. I could talk with these young men about their lives and their problems because I had experienced it myself.

Talking with those young men, spending time volunteering as a mentor, was truly a major changing point in my life. Looking back now, I can see that when God took away all those things I once thought were important in my life, He forced me to look inside myself and find my true purpose in life, my reason for existence. In other words, I had to learn something new about myself. Up until that point, I thought the journey was all about achieving things, checking off the boxes on my list of what I wanted to get out of life. I had devalued relationships and looked at people as dispensable, as something there to help me get along in my journey. But talking with those guys—having authentic conversations— showed me I had missed what was really important in life, and that was the relationships. It was all about being a good son, husband, friend, and father. Spending time as a mentor helped show me that, for me, fulfillment comes when I invest in people.

Eventually I did get another job, one that took me to a new city. I had to leave the guys in that start-up mentoring program. But as soon as I got settled into my new place, more opportunities to connect with others and build relationships fell into my lap. Seemingly out of the blue one day I got a call from a career counselor at a local high school to come speak to a few classes and share my experiences. That helped get me started volunteering in my new community, talking with young people and working with them to make a positive change in their lives.

That time when I was out of work was such a transformational time for me. It gave me time to discover who I was, and most importantly, the time allowed me to learn something new about myself and discover my *why*. That time really forced me to look in the mirror and evaluate the quality of my relationships. I began to truly understand my purpose in life: to help young men build a purpose-driven foundation for their lives. All of the other things, like the career and the house, fell into place because I then had a purpose and true vision of where I was going in life. I understood that fulfillment for me would come from investing in other people.

IN ORDER TO TRULY BE FULFILLED, YOU ALSO NEED TO UNDERSTAND YOUR WHY. YOU HAVE TO TAKE TIME TO THINK ABOUT WHAT IT IS THAT MAKES YOU HAPPY AND FULFILLED.

In this book, we've talked about realizing the need for change in your life, developing a plan to make that happen, and finding the courage to take those first steps toward your goals. Those are all important steps, and they help you understand what it is you want out of life. But in order to truly be fulfilled, you also need to understand your why. You have to take time to think about what it is that makes you happy and fulfilled. For me, it is investing time in helping other people by sharing my experiences, but it might be something different for you. There are many different ways to serve others.

So how do you find out your why, your passion in life? It takes a lot of self-discovery and evaluation. It takes asking yourself, "What am I passionate about? What type of advice do people gravitate to me for?" But it also takes looking around you and paying attention to the people who are in your life. There are people in our lives who have advice for us and can teach us valuable lessons if only we are open to them and listen to what they have to say.

One person who really triggered a change in me, who wasn't even in my life for very long, was that career counselor. By asking how he could help me, he was encouraging me to think of how I could help myself. If I had let pride stand in my way and not listened to this person, I wouldn't have found that first opportunity to volunteer and give my time to helping others.

Look at your own life and the people in it. Think about your teachers, your friends, your parents, and people of influence. Ask yourself, "Why are they there? Am I listening to what they're saying?"

Then also take a long, hard look at yourself. What is it that makes you happy? What would you do with your life if money weren't an issue?

Once you understand the why behind who you are and what your goals are, it makes it easier to write your master plan. You have a clearer picture of where you're going because you know why it is you want to go there.

And remember that you can find ways to serve in many different places. I had a conversation with a young man one time who was in college majoring in finance. "How will that type of career help me serve others?" he asked. I offered some suggestions, such as helping people become more financially literate or helping people find financial security. The motivation for what you're doing with your life shouldn't be the money. It should be about the good you can do. Ask yourself, "How can I serve others in this capacity?"

When you understand your own why, the part of you that makes you unique and fulfilled, the master plan will fall into place. When you take time to understand why you exist, what your passions are, and what your purpose is in life, it helps in making other decisions, such as which college to go to or what career path to take. Once you understand what your passions are, your true reasons for existing, you can align all of those things with whatever setting you want to be in.

Remember that the power to change is within you. You are the only person who can truly understand where your passions lie. And you are the only person who can take the steps to change your life, to take it in the direction you want it to go.

choose
your why

Understand the why and reasons for making those resolutions in the first place. In other words, understand the foundation of the entire change process that will have a domino effect on your life.

talk
about
it

Don't keep your resolution a secret. Tell friends and family members who will be there to support your resolve to change yourself for the better or improve your health.

focus on the habits,
not the outcome

Focus on the habits that will eventually become second nature. Making long-lasting changes are more beneficial than a short-term fix.

Write your "who am I" statement here.

_____

_____

_____

_____

What three habits (positive or negative)
do I find myself repeating most often?

1 _____

2 _____

3 _____

What are the three things that most excite me?

1 _____

2 _____

3 _____

What three things would I do if money weren't an issue?

1 _____

2 _____

3 _____

ALLOWING OURSELVES TO INDULGE IN OUR CURIOSITY CAN HELP US DISCOVER NEW SKILLS AND IDEAS THAT CAN HAVE LASTING IMPACTS ON OUR LIVES.

Stay Curious:
Great Things Come from Unexpected Places

This year, I resolve to stay curious about the incredible world that we live in and continue to ask plenty of questions each day. I resolve to learn new things and stay informed and aware of global issues. I will write letters about curious topics, sign petitions, speak at public events, attend rallies, make phone calls, and spread the word about problems that need attention. I will remain curious for causes I am passionate about: the environment, education, sustainability, organic farming, and social justice. I will even volunteer for causes that I'm not as familiar with; I feel that I am my best self when I am learning something new and serving my community.

Many of us begin the year with many of these same thoughts. But not wanting our curiosity to come off too aggressively or as ignorance, we end up listening passively and not engaging experts with our questions. Or we research a topic quietly on the Internet but don't act on the knowledge we gain. Or we overthink what people have to say and end up with "analysis paralysis."

Think about it: as kids we're insatiably inquisitive. Everything—from pets to skyrockets to dirt to our own hands—fascinates us. But for many of us, as we begin to grow older, we lose our desire for curiosity. And yet curiosity is powerful. Many researchers have proved that it adds color, vibrancy, passion, and pleasure to our lives. It helps us solve unusual problems. It helps us do better in our daily lives. And even more so, it is our birthright as Ian Leslie writes in his book *Curious: The Desire to Know and Why Your Future Depends on It*.

AS KIDS WE'RE INSATIABLY INQUISITIVE. EVERYTHING—FROM PETS TO SKYROCKETS TO DIRT TO OUR OWN HANDS—FASCINATES US. BUT FOR MANY OF US, AS WE START GETTING OLDER, WE LOSE OUR DESIRE FOR CURIOSITY.

Take the inventors of the Android operating system (OS) that powers 86 percent of smartphones today. In a 2018 article titled "The History of Android OS: Its Name, Origin and More" on androidauthority.com, columnist John Callaham wrote about how Android evolved. The company was founded in 2003 (four years before iPhones were launched) and began developing software to wirelessly connect digital cameras to PCs and to cloud servers to store photos (three years before companies began pushing for consumer-based cloud storage applications). Soon after, the company's founders realized the declining stand-alone digital camera market would not offer its product a viable future. So they decided to focus the software on mobile phones instead. In 2005, Google acquired Android, and the Android founders continued development for Google. They based their development on the open-source Linux system, which meant other companies could have free access to the code to build mobile phones and apps. Imagine if the Android founders never let their curiosity roam freely regarding other uses of their technology? Where would the smartphone industry be today?

My own curiosity once led me on an adventure in the snow. It was a typical winter day in Detroit, and I couldn't seem to get going. Taking a deep breath, I tried again, slowly lifting my foot from the clutch. The combination of icy road and an anything-but-smooth takeoff into first gear made the car seem like it was heaving and coughing versus smoothly driving. Regardless of how embarrassing the event was, it was my first actual takeoff in first gear. The celebratory smile only lasted for a few seconds after I quickly realized that I was coming to a stop sign requiring me to brake, look both ways for oncoming cars, steer in snow, press the clutch, and remain aware of my surroundings.

This was my first day driving my newly purchased car. It was a hatchback Ford Escort with a five-speed transmission that I had purchased for $900 from a neighbor. Somehow the pride of purchasing my own car overshadowed the fact that I didn't know how to drive a manual transmission. My driving coach, the neighbor that I purchased the car from, asked, "Would you like to know how this car works? It may give you a better understanding of what you're doing."

Agreeing to pull the car over in the middle of the winter

would be the turning point. Lifting the hood of the car, I curiously stared at the engine not exactly understanding what I was looking at. Jim, my coach, said, "Think of it like changing gears on a bicycle, every time you need to go faster, you'll need to change gears." Over the next three to four minutes I stared at the engine trying to put in place the things that Jim taught me about driving the manual transmission.

Learning how to drive a manual transmission taught me many life lessons! First, I learned that you don't have to fully understand something before committing to it; the fear of not knowing how to drive the car could have kept me from buying the car at such a valuable price. Second, my curiosity of learning to associate different experiences would be the biggest payoff from the lesson. Comparing the gear mechanism with the bike was the first step in the process. Learning how to prioritize and sequence a series of important tasks was the biggest lesson. My curiosity and ability to visualize important steps in a process created a sense of understanding that I use today.

I LEARNED THAT YOU DON'T HAVE TO FULLY UNDERSTAND SOMETHING BEFORE COMMITTING TO IT.

Take for example the curiosity we all have as kids and the lessons that we've carried for years and applied to our daily lives. It could be how to balance blocks or critically think through a Rubik's Cube—those skills help us in many aspects of our live. Think about the creators of Android. What would have happened if they didn't allow their curiosity to apply their newly created digital camera software to be used in an early version of a smartphone.

Allowing ourselves to indulge in our curiosity can help us discover new skills and ideas that can have lasting impacts on our lives. The next time you try to talk yourself out of trying a new food, book, conversation, or simply engaging in a discussion with someone who doesn't look like you, remember to allow the curious side of you to engage. You never know what you'll learn about yourself, the other person, or the world around you.

ask why

Become the "question person," asking questions for clarity and learning. Sometimes we don't ask why because we simply assume we know the answer. Don't worry about coming across as stupid. Asking the small—yet big—question "Why?" can have powerful results.

be a thinkerer

The term "thinkerer" was created by mixing "think" and "tinker." Ian Leslie uses it to mean "a style of cognitive investigation that mixes the concrete and the abstract, toggling between the details and the big picture, zooming out to see the woods and back in again to examine the bark on the tree.

consume content that's outside of your comfort zone

Whether you focus on productivity habits, Egyptian pyramids, beer brewing, or something entirely different is up to you. The important part is that the content is unfamiliar—basic research will spur you to want to know more. When we don't have any initial knowledge about something, we're not really curious about it—that is, until we have to be.

Stay Curious
Personal Contract

I, _____ , do hereby agree to stay curious and explore at least one new "thing" each month. That "thing" could be a place, topic, or skill. I will use the following resources to help me explore:

The library: _____ Date: _____

The Internet: _____ Date: _____

My educators and mentors: _____ Date: _____

My own two legs: _____ Date: _____

Signed: _____ Date: _____

Witnessed: _____ Date: _____

Write down some things you already know you want to explore.

_____   _____

_____   _____

_____   _____

_____   _____

MEETING NEW PEOPLE WITH FRESH PERSPECTIVES CAN HELP GENERATE NEW IDEAS.

CHAPTER 6

Meet New People:
Permission to Be

Throughout the course of the year, it is easy to get stuck in a rut. The mundane tasks of living life can suck us into a routine that isn't necessarily a part of the resolution to become more productive, more connected or to live life differently. We start the year full of energy motivated to live out the goals that we've established. Unfortunately, by the time June rolls around, we usually end up staying at home, missing out on a lot of interesting opportunities to learn new things, to experience new and interesting foods or culture, or simply to connect and have fun. However, meeting new people can be the welcome change necessary and inject a new and welcome energy into our daily routines. Introducing new personalities into our lives can break the routine and can be beneficial to our mental, spiritual, and physical well-being.

In addition to the immediate benefits, meeting new people can be the key to landing a new career, getting the most from your classes, or figuring out the last line of code. The physical world is a beautiful place and deserves to be explored outside of our digital networks of friends. Don't wait for permission to be a friend, spend some of your free time at the nearest coffee shop, take a class at a home improvement store, or join your city's most interesting Meetup.com group. Don't be afraid to get out there and make some new friends, overcome your shyness, get some knowledge, and get to know interesting people.

After spending seven years of my young adult life in the Army, it was time to make a decision about my future: do I reenlist or enter the civilian world? There were several benefits associated with either decision. Many of my Army buddies opted to stay in, but my decision was final—I knew it was time for me to move on to the next chapter for my life.

My years in the Army were great. Signing up had given me the opportunity to expand my perspective and explore the world, and it offered the needed change I had been looking for. I also had the opportunity to live in places I didn't even know existed as a kid from Detroit. I grew as a person because of the exposure to new cultures and saw different ways of living than I had experienced in the neighborhood where I grew up.

But it was time to move on. I have always loved to learn and been a very curious person—asking questions and trying to find answers to things—and it was time to broaden my horizons once again and keep moving forward with my journey. There were opportunities available in the civilian world that I didn't see as an option in the military, so I decided not to reenlist when the time came. It was time to use the leadership experience from the Army and build on it. I just wasn't totally clear what that meant at the time.

My first step after leaving the Army was to apply to college. It felt like a logical step, and I'd been taught that going to college was what successful people did, so it seemed natural. After years at a foodservice-supply chain and a line cook in the Army, I decided to apply to Johnson & Wales culinary school. I enjoyed the fast-paced world inside the kitchen, and it seemed like the next logical step. After all, working in the kitchen was what I knew. Unfortunately, halfway through the program, a nagging military injury resulted in reconstructive foot surgery and meant my life would take a different path. When the doctor told me that I wouldn't be able to stand for more than eight hours at a time, I realized I couldn't continue with the career path I thought I was on. After taking a step back and evaluating my options, I transferred to the University of South Carolina and began to work on a business degree. The opportunities that business school could unlock were vague, similar to my dreams. I knew I wanted to find a different path in life compared to what I'd experienced in Detroit, but I still wasn't sure what that would shape up to be.

Once I settled into my course work, I began looking for a job. I have always worked and needed to support myself even while I was going to college. I responded to an ad in the local paper to work for the world's largest soft drink provider and accepted an offer shortly after.

I joined the sales team and was excited to put in my time working in the trenches, so to speak. As part of the sales team, I showed up for meetings at 5 a.m. We'd pick up our sales call list, get briefed on new promotions, and hit the road. I would see about ten to fifteen store managers a day, of the 200 or so in my region, talking with people, negotiating pricing, and informing them of the opportunities to increase their sales, which in turn helped me earn a larger commission check. Then around 5 p.m. I called it a day and shifted to student mode. I'd study and go to classes from 6 to 11 p.m., before hitting the bed, exhausted, only to start all over again at the crack of dawn the next morning.

After a while, I started to get frustrated. I was working hard, and my sales numbers were great. But when I looked around me, I saw other people getting promoted, and I hadn't been promoted yet. What was wrong? I'd always been taught if you work hard and do your best, someone will notice. But that strategy didn't seem to be working here. I couldn't figure out how I could be putting in ten to twelve hours per day, coming in as one of the top performers, and still not getting promoted.

One day, right after our region got a new general manager who was a huge South Carolina Gamecock fan, I randomly introduced myself as a fellow fan. After a few interactions regarding business performance, he asked me to look over some financial reports. I took the spreadsheets home, analyzed them, and brought them to him on Monday morning. Surprised by the quality of my work, he gave me a year's worth of records to analyze, and I did the same thing. The seemingly random introduction was the beginning of a longstanding working relationship between me and the general manager. He respected my work, and I was able to show I had skillsets beyond selling. So one day, when we were talking, I decided to just be frank. He could sense my frustration, and he asked what was going on.

"I'm going to be honest with you," I said. "I look around and see guys out there getting promoted, moving up, and they're not producing at the same rate as I am. What's the deal?"

"You can do whatever you want to do, Reginald; no one's stopping you," he said.

"I understand that, but what's next for me?"

"You're talented and ambitious, you tell me what's next," he said.

I still didn't get it. I was looking for a promotion from one job to the other, something clear and well defined. But he just kept telling me these vague statements that I could do whatever I wanted. One day, his words finally sunk in.

"Reginald, you tell me where you want to go, and I'll help you get there."

My general manager was giving me the tools and platform to get where I wanted in my career. The thing was, I had to figure out where that was going to be. I had a dream since I was a kid of a general direction I wanted to go in life. I knew I wanted out of Detroit. I knew I wanted opportunities to make my life stable and secure and to provide for my family when I had one. But I had never really thought about where that was taking me until that conversation with my boss.

He gave me permission to do whatever I wanted to do. So now it was time to figure that out. This was all new to me. I learned I have control over my career, just like I have control over my life. Learning that I could dictate what I wanted, where I wanted my career to go, opened up a whole new world of opportunity. It was a defining point for me.

And it wasn't just a title or position that I needed to settle on. It was time to decide what type of leader I wanted to be and what type of person. What did I want other people to think of when they heard the name Reginald Bean?

Just like the decision I made to change my life's direction and get out of Detroit, this realization that I could be whoever I wanted was empowering but had its hurdles. Knowing I wanted to be a strong, competent, respected leader was one thing. Becoming one was going to take time.

I'll never forget the first time I had to make a presentation for our annual sales meeting. When I was first given the project, I was excited. It was my time to shine, to show others what I could do and share my ideas and vision for the company. I had watched dozens of these presentations delivered before. The person would get up, tell a few jokes, and captivate the crowd. They made it look so easy, and I figured I could do the same thing. But when the time came, I froze like a deer in headlights. I looked at that room of 300 people, and my palms started to sweat, and my mouth got dry. I started in on my presentation, which was only about ten slides, a thirty-minute presentation, but it felt like three hours. I didn't have water with me, I didn't know how to put the crowd at ease, I didn't have anything prepared other than what was on the slides, and I realized, too late, that wasn't enough.

That experience, fumbling through a presentation in front of a large crowd, taught me that there was a lot of preparation that goes into being an effective communicator and also into being a good leader. After my conversation with my general manager, I knew where I wanted to go. Now it was time to work on the steps it would take to get there.

I learned a lot in those first years on the job, but the most important thing I learned is we have permission to be whatever type of person we want to be. We have the power to decide, and we can't let the expectations of others decide for us. What kind of father or mother do you want to be? What kind of student do you want to be? What kind of employee, leader, or athlete do you want to be? You have permission to be whatever you decide; it is up to you to fill in the blank.

I'm not talking just about what job you want here. I'm talking about what kind of person you want to be. What do you want people to think of when they think of you?

Take a good hard look at yourself in the mirror. Who do you see? Who do you want to see? Is there someone in your life who can help you get there? When was the last time you met someone new—someone who can help you sort through ideas and thoughts or maybe the directions for your journey?

WE ALL NEED HELP GETTING TO THE NEXT CHAPTER IN OUR LIVES.

Here's what I've learned: regardless of your dreams and ambitions, we all need help getting to the next chapter in our lives. Meeting new people with fresh perspectives can help generate new ideas; however, the decision to be is up to you. You'll have to decide what you want out of life—the type of father, friend, partner, or employee that you want to be. Once you've made the decision, those you trust can help you get there.

change your behavior over time

Unproductive behaviors develop over the course of time. Replacing these behaviors with healthy ones requires time. Don't get overwhelmed and think that you have to reassess everything in your life.

ask for support

Accepting help from those who care about you and will listen strengthens your resilience and ability to manage stress caused by your resolution.

pick a start date

You don't have to make these changes on New Year's Day.

This month's goal targets are:

_____

_____

_____

_____

Three behaviors I can adopt to replace unproductive ones:

1 _____

_____

_____

2 _____

_____

_____

3 _____

_____

_____

SOMETIMES WE NEED A BIGGER NUDGE THAN JUST TURNING THE CALENDAR INTO A NEW YEAR.

Earn More Money:
Some Things
Money Can Buy

Many of us are looking for ways to improve our lives, but sometimes we need a bigger nudge than just turning the calendar into a new year. Some of our improvements center around our mental, physical, or financial well-being. For the most part, we combine some tips and assistance from our favorite apps or websites to help us achieve our goals, which often center around our finances, in order to sort through our lives.

When it comes to money, however, setting New Year's resolutions to earn more is easy, but developing a plan, committing to, and following through with those resolutions is a completely different story. Many future plans are dependent on an increase in extra income, which means saving more or making more, and putting a focus on setting realistic and achievable financial goals. There is hardly a quicker way to deflate your New Year's resolutions than to realize that they are unattainable or that you've set the bar so high that only Mark Zuckerberg himself could achieve them.

Earning a little extra income can be a wonderful financial resolution. Regardless of whether you're a new graduate or in a sluggish economy, the peace of mind and extra income that comes with a new job, second job, or side business can be a great buffer against the stresses of life. An extra couple hundred dollars a month can also be a great way to reach financial goals like paying down debt, starting a business, or increasing an emergency fund. And that requires a budget.

Starting off the year with a budget is an easy resolution that can be completed while binge watching the latest show on Netflix or relaxing at the park. Your budget doesn't have to be in a fancy spreadsheet with graphs and charts. A simple, handwritten list of expenses and incomes can get you started and can be expanded later if needed.

The hard part of this resolution is committing yourself to monitoring, modifying, and managing your budget over the course of the year. Consider using a financial app to keep your budget in an easy to access place so that it will be a constant reminder of your financial goals and your commitment to those goals.

Even with our plan to earn extra money, there are some things on your list that money can't buy, as I found out on April 1, 2002, when my life changed forever.

I held a little, four-pound, twelve-ounce baby in my arms—my daughter, Arden. She looked up at me with amazingly beautiful eyes, and my heart was filled with a love like I'd never experienced before.

The two hours leading to her birth were filled with an amazing emotional roller coaster considering she wasn't expected to arrive for another eight weeks. Of course, I was expecting Arden and had plenty of time to mentally prepare, but all of a sudden, a wave of doubt filled my thoughts. I wondered if I were really ready. Did I have what it took to be a father, to be a protector?

Once her little eyes connected with mine, my entire way of thinking changed in an instant. I was filled with so much love for her that from that point on, every decision I made would be to do the best I could for her.

For the first time in my life, I felt real, unconditional love—the kind of love that you can't describe but you know you'll do everything and give up anything to protect it. However, that joyful feeling quickly turned to confusion and frustration. Why was this the first time I felt unconditional love? Why did I have this feeling of love for my daughter, but I didn't have that same feeling of love for myself?

If you'd asked anyone in my circle at that time in my life if I was happy with myself, they would have answered with a confident yes. Here's the deal: I'd become an expert at projecting—projecting confidence, projecting security and intellect. I hid the insecure parts of me I thought wouldn't be acceptable to the world and only let people know things about me that I thought would make me look better in their eyes. I projected a sense of swagger that comes with finding success, and I knew how to present myself well.

> I HID THE INSECURE PARTS OF ME I THOUGHT WOULDN'T BE ACCEPTABLE TO THE WORLD AND ONLY LET PEOPLE KNOW THINGS ABOUT ME THAT I THOUGHT WOULD MAKE ME LOOK BETTER IN THEIR EYES.

But inside I was miserable and filled with self-doubt. I might have been able to project confidence, but I really didn't like who I was at all, let alone love myself.

This ability to project an outward confidence was something I had learned early in my life as a means of self-preservation. The adolescent years of a child's life are extremely important, for fathers play significant roles in the emotional and psychological development. Unfortunately, mine wasn't around much. When I got to middle school and had my first real crush on a girl, I didn't have a father to turn to. I didn't have anyone to ask questions about what I should do and how I should talk to her. When I was assigned a project in high school that felt overwhelming, I didn't have a father at home to help me break it down and tackle it. I had to figure these things out by myself or stumble my way through it, and that gave me a false sense of confidence. It was easy to think I didn't need a dad when I was able to get through the struggles of growing up without him with minimal scars. I wanted to think that I was self-reliant and projected an outwardly confidence, but I didn't like who I was on the inside.

When I didn't necessarily fit in with other kids in the neighborhood, I didn't have a dad at home to back me up and tell me the things I liked were okay. This made me feel like the things I liked weren't good enough and that my way of thinking about things or reacting to things wasn't the way it should be. I started to hide them from others and only project a person who I thought would get accepted.

I received unconditional and nurturing love from my mom and grandmother, but I was missing the security and reinforcement from my dad. I started to have a lot of insecurities, and those insecurities turned into things I didn't like about myself. Even though I was able to project self-confidence, on the inside I was filled with insecurity and doubt, and that turned into anger. I was mad at the world for the situation I had been born into and for not having the opportunities I thought I deserved.

I RECEIVED UNCONDITIONAL AND NURTURING LOVE FROM MY MOM AND GRANDMOTHER, BUT I WAS MISSING THE SECURITY AND REINFORCEMENT FROM MY DAD.

This is my story, but I know I am not alone. I see this same outward confidence in other young people, but I can so easily see that inside they are filled with insecurity and self-doubt. It affects how we behave and the decisions we make. If you don't love yourself and who you are, it is easier to make decisions to do things that might hurt yourself or your body. Promiscuous behavior, fighting, doing drugs and alcohol—all of these are ways of acting out when we don't love who we are.

What I did was try to overcompensate for the lack of like for myself with material things, thinking if I look the part then maybe I'll feel the part. I got a decent job to support the things that I needed to buy in order to feel good about myself. As a young adult, I thought if I buy this car or this house, others wouldn't see that I was hurting inside, and it distracted me from how I truly felt about myself. But nothing that is material can change how I felt about myself on the inside. Just as the power to change comes from within, the power to love comes from within too.

It's the same for all of us. Before we can love others, before we can be who we truly want to be in life, we have to first learn to love who we are. We have to come to terms with who we are on the inside, to love ourselves—quirks and all—and be willing to share it with the world. Regardless of our attempts to cover up, hide, or camouflage who we are, there are simply some things that money can't buy.

When you try to hide your real self because of insecurities, it takes energy and effort to keep up "the face." All the time I spent trying to be someone I wasn't was taking time away from being who I was. When I became a father, I had a little more motivation to be the person I was designed to be. I held that reason in my arms, looking into her eyes, and I promised her the world. I had an overwhelming sense of "I can be who I am," plus I knew that this little lady might call me out if she saw a conflict in behavior. Embracing the authentic me felt great. Letting go of my insecurities allowed space for me to embrace myself and move forward.

I found out that the more I revealed about myself, the more I was able to shed those insecurities and be true to my personality and characteristics, the better relationships I had with everyone in my life, whether it was family or work. And I realized this was something I needed to do in order to be the best father to Arden. Making the decision to embrace and love myself helped propel me forward in a new way. I had permission to be whatever I wanted to be in life, but before I could truly make that happen, I had to learn to love who I was on the inside.

YOU HAVE PERMISSION TO BE WHATEVER YOU WANT, BUT BEFORE YOU CAN GET THERE, YOU HAVE TO LEARN TO LOVE YOURSELF.

The same is true for you. You have permission to be whatever you want, but before you can get there, you have to learn to love yourself. All you can do is be who you are. If you are constantly trying to change who you are to fit other people's expectations or to be like people you think are successful, you will never win. You can't win by being someone else. It goes the other way too. If anyone is trying to be better than you by being like you, they'll never win. The only way to win in life is by being true to yourself. It's just a fact: no one can beat you at being you.

This all comes back around to how many of us focus on adding more money as our New Year's resolutions as a way to solve other issues in our lives. The truth is, the lack of money is a by-product of much broader issues in our lives. As many have found, we can't hide behind "stuff" forever. Eventually, we'll have to look ourselves in the mirror and embrace the skin that we're in. My advice, the next time you find yourself saying you need more money or more stuff, ask yourself if you're overcompensating for something? Are you buying something new as a way to project a certain image or façade?

keep trying

If you have totally run out of steam when it comes to keeping your resolution by mid-February, don't despair. Start over again! Recommit yourself for twenty-four hours.

just pick one thing

If you want to change your life or your lifestyle, don't try to change the whole thing at once. Instead, pick one area of your life to change to begin with.

plan ahead

Plan for success—get everything ready, so things will run smoothly. If you're taking up running, make sure you have things in place to help you succeed.

What are the insecurities that you try to hide.?

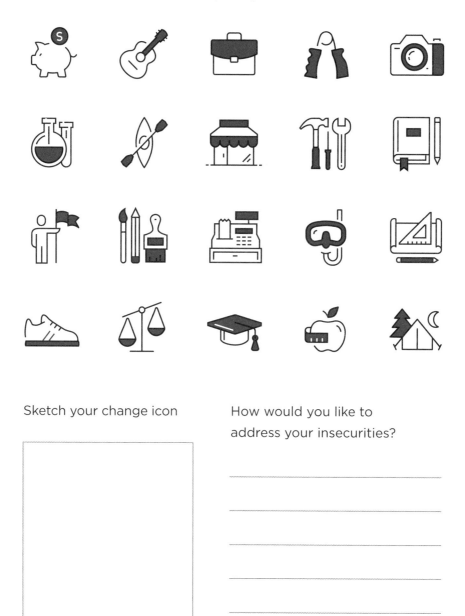

Sketch your change icon

How would you like to
address your insecurities?

WHAT ARE OUR EVER-INCREASING DIGITAL LIVES DOING TO OUR PERSONALITIES AND MENTAL WELL-BEING?

CHAPTER 8

Spend Less Time on Social Media:
Love Your Selfie

J ust one final tweet, like, post, or comment, then I'm preparing for a digital detox! This story may be familiar to many of us because we've lived it. We commit to starting our year by kicking our social media habits in favor of more face time with our friends and family.

The story of Mark Zuckerberg, the rise of Facebook, and the one billion users heavily engaging in the platform daily, along with creating an entirely new media outlet, is well documented. There is also the success that social media has had disrupting the advertising business, creating a new and more cost-effective way to advertise traditional brands, becoming a true American story. There are, however, adverse reactions to the success of social media.

Occasionally, I've heard stories of people, young and old, addicted to social media creating an artificial bridge between their physical and digital lives. Research reveals that the outcome of these addictions has led to depression, cyberbullying, and other perils of living a constantly wired life. What are our ever-increasing digital lives doing to our personalities and mental well-being?

One of the most compelling books that I've read this year, *Alone Together* by Sherry Turkle, reminds us that technology promises to let us do anything from anywhere with anyone. But it also drains us as we try to do everything everywhere. We begin to feel overwhelmed and depleted by what technology makes possible. We may be free to work from anywhere, but we are also prone to being lonely everywhere. In a surprising twist, relentless connection leads to a new solitude. We turn to new technology to fill the void, but as technology ramps up, our emotional lives ramp down—alone together.

Being a social media user on multiple platforms, I'm often reminded that communication technologies can permeate my life really quickly. I often neglect to stop and ask myself whether I am using these technologies in a healthy, productive, and socially acceptable manner—one that allows me to stay connected to my physical world without impacting my views or how I respect and love myself while I'm comparing my post to someone else.

When I was younger, far before these digital platforms existed, I had an experience similar to the emotional detachment common in today's social media. Back when I was eight or nine years old, I had one obsession. It wasn't learning a new trick on my bike or getting a new GI Joe figure. I obsessed with the thought of spending time with my dad. I wanted to walk like he walked, dress like he dressed, speak with the same cadence and slang that he used, but most importantly I wanted to learn what it meant to be an adult—you know, a responsible man. Who better to learn from than my own dad, right? Here's the dilemma: my parents were divorced, and I spent 99.9 percent of my time with my mom or one of her three sisters. I saw these women work hard every day to provide for their families, doing shift work to provide the basic necessities. At a young age, I realized that I wanted more than simply the basic necessities; I craved emotional and psychological support. I wanted to see what Dad did, what type of work he did, how he talked to other men. I just wanted to be around him.

But as much as I wished to spend time with my dad, the occasions where we would spend time together were pretty rare. Sometimes he'd call up during the week and tell my mom he would pick me up and spend time with me during the upcoming weekend. In preparation for his arrival, I'd pack a bag and sit at the window watching for him way before the time that he promised. Then I'd wait … and wait … and wait. The hours ticked by slowly. Noon turned to 3:00, then 3:00 to 6:00. I would give up my post at the window and go off to hide my disappointment. Maybe sometime around 9:00 he'd call my mom and tell her he wasn't going to make it. My young mind had figured it out already.

As I grew older, I worked hard to hide how I truly felt about the constant disappointment, and acted tough and began to entertain behaviors that weren't truly me in order to redirect my true emotions. But time after time the same thing would happen. I would spend the afternoon waiting on my dad, who never showed up. I started to think he really didn't like me, and that's why he didn't want to be around me. Maybe I wasn't good enough for him, not smart or funny or tough enough. So I tried to be different. Similar to today's social media trends, I tried to make myself into someone that I thought my dad would like better.

I created my own story. If my dad didn't love me for who I was, maybe no one else did either. And eventually, I started to reject who I really was. I didn't love the quirks about me that made my personality unique. I didn't love the fact that I was a compassionate person who was interested in learning useless information. But I didn't love the person I was pretending to be either.

In the previous chapters, I talked about how in order to be successful you have to be happy with your choices and with who you are. But the key to being happy with who you are means accepting who you are and loving yourself first. It means figuring out all those quirks of your personality that you've suppressed over the years, thinking they're not accepted by others, and letting them shine through. It means digging deep within you to learn what you really like to do with your time and what you really want to be in life and then embracing it fully.

I DIDN'T LOVE THE QUIRKS ABOUT ME THAT MADE MY PERSONALITY UNIQUE.

For me, learning to love and accept myself didn't come until I was a young adult. I looked in the mirror one day and realized I'm all I've got in the world—me. My years in the military provided a lot of time to think and reflect not on who I wanted to be but on who I actually was. When we were out on long missions, I had a lot of time to be alone with nothing really to do except wait until my next shift. I realized I liked reading, loved learning, and had a passion to solve problems, and that there's absolutely nothing wrong with that. I had an overwhelming sense of self-acceptance. It was exhilarating, and I felt complete.

It turns out, it was exhausting being someone I wasn't. I had spent my life trying to live up to others expectations of whom I thought they wanted me to be, trying to figure out what I could do to make my dad love me and what I thought I needed to do to make other people love me, when all along the secret to unlocking my potential was learning to love myself.

Learning to love yourself is a process, especially for someone like me who grew up with mixed messages. I felt unloved by the person whom I needed love from the most, who decided not to take the time to show up when he said he would on a Saturday. In order to love myself, I had to take that praise and reinforcement from the positive influences in my life and embrace it and let myself believe it was true. I also had to evaluate my own values and personality traits and accept myself for who I was. It was all a matter of figuring out how to embrace me, to compare myself to my own potential rather than comparing myself to others.

Figuring out who you are and the impact you'd like to make in life is the important first step in loving yourself. Whether that's figuring out you want to be known as a good guy, someone who's dependable, or figuring out what type of career you want, knowing the goal you're striving toward is an important step. But once you've figured that out, you have to learn to love yourself in order to get there. Finding success in life and becoming the person you truly want to be can never happen unless you love yourself for who you are first.

FIGURING OUT WHO YOU ARE AND THE IMPACT YOU'D LIKE TO MAKE IN LIFE IS THE IMPORTANT FIRST STEP IN LOVING YOURSELF.

It's similar to taking a selfie with the perfect angle and fictitious backdrop, then looking at the picture with a not-so-excited look. We flip through the appropriate filters and touch up the blemishes that we don't approve of, and then we smile! The picture is ready to share with the world with a cheesy caption about that particular moment in life. But is this really life? Or is this the life we want people to think we're living—the life with no blemishes or flaws and with the perfect backdrop? What would happen if we posted pictures without any filters in our own living rooms with realistic captions?

For me, posting my unfiltered picture came in phases. Learning to love myself was a process. It started first in my years in the Army when I realized it was just too much work to pretend to be someone I wasn't. I started to let myself do things I liked and let my personality shine through, and I learned that the more I revealed about myself, the better relationships I had. It only makes sense that by being true to yourself, you will have strong relationships built on trust and acceptance.

IT ONLY MAKES SENSE THAT BY BEING TRUE TO YOURSELF, YOU WILL HAVE STRONG RELATIONSHIPS BUILT ON TRUST AND ACCEPTANCE.

Think about it like you would looking at a selfie on your phone. Your first instinct might be to say, "Man, look at that double chin," or "I wish I had different hair." Rather than focusing on the negative, turn it into a positive like, "I love my smile," or "My eyes are looking particularly bright and cheerful today."

Then think of your inner self, your personality, as your selfie. Embrace your quirks and unique personality traits. Try to stop being negative toward yourself and pretending to be someone you're not in order to please others. Instead, focus on the positive and reinforce those positives on a daily basis. Pretty soon you'll love yourself for who you are, and you'll be on your way to becoming a happy, confident, and successful person.

connect with a compelling why

For your resolution to stick, it must be aligned with your core values and hold deep, personal meaning that you connect with on a deep, emotional level

narrow your focus

Start with just one major undertaking come January 1st. Then break that goal down into doable, small, bite-size steps.

expect setbacks

What matters most isn't that everything goes exactly to plan; it's what you do when it doesn't!

WRITE YOUR PERSONAL MISSION STATEMENT

A personal mission statement briefly summarizes your guiding principles. It should be short enough to memorize. Repeat it to yourself as you're making important decisions. Ask yourself these questions to help you form your personal mission:

1 What values are most important to me?

2 What does my ideal self look like?

3 What impact do I want to make on the people around me? On the world?

WE HAVE A TENDENCY TO LIVE OUR LIVES BASED ON OTHER PEOPLE'S EXPECTATIONS OF US, WHETHER THOSE EXPECTATIONS ARE GOOD OR BAD.

Break the
Smartphone Addiction:
The Pygmalion Effect

A t this point in the year, many of us have made personal commitments and resolutions to change or enhance some portion of our lives. The wonderful thing is many of us have seen significant changes from the commitments we've made throughout the year. Unfortunately, for others the excitement has worn off, and old habits began to creep in, particularly the uneasy and sometimes all-consuming feeling that we've missed out on something as a result of our changes—what our friends are doing, in the know about, or in possession of something more or better. The fear of missing out, or FOMO as it's commonly referred to, is defined by the *Oxford Dictionary* (online US version) as "an anxiety that an exciting or interesting event may currently be happening elsewhere, often aroused by posts seen on a social media website."

For many of us, our FOMO is a result of an addiction to our smartphones. You know that small but powerful device that

Revealing Your Full Potential through Purpose and Perspective | **91** gives us access to a world of information. Our smartphones give us access to entire bodies of research, multiple versions of dictionaries around the world as well as useful and beneficial medical research. Unfortunately, that same device can also give us full access to our friends and family lives via multiple social media platforms. This all access encourages many of us to check our phone every 2-5 minutes making it a matter of life and death that we respond, like, retweet or repost regardless if you are on Facebook, Twitter of Snap Chat, social media has created a sense of urgency and anxiety for many people.

We can accept the smartphone addition or FOMO as part of behavior from the adolescence or young adults in our lives; however, as we grow into adults, we assume that we will mature and grow out of the behavior. But the growth continues, and the stakes are raised. No longer is it about likes and retweets, it is about keeping up with the Joneses and rushing to chase a dream script that outlines what a "perfect adult life" entails. This usually involves a spouse you are madly in love with, an upwardly mobile career at a solid start-up tech company, 2.5 kids, and a car no more than a few years old. FOMO can derail progress made and force us to live our lives based on expectations from others.

FOMO CAN DERAIL PROGRESS MADE AND FORCE US TO LIVE OUR LIVES BASED ON EXPECTATIONS FROM OTHERS.

I remember a hot day in Detroit—one of those days in May that feels like summer has already arrived, but it hadn't yet. I was sitting in class at Cooley High School trying to stay focused on what my teacher was saying. My high school was a historic building in Detroit, which meant not only did it have beautiful architecture that went unappreciated by the hordes of students walking through the halls every day, but also it didn't have air conditioning. So on this day, like many others, I was sitting by an open window where the noise of the street fought for my attention: the people talking, the cars going by, and the random police sirens.

All of a sudden, a couple of police cars pulled up. I noticed but didn't pay much attention. We had a lot of fights at my school, and it wasn't unusual for the police to show up. But then an ambulance joined the emergency vehicles. By now, I had completely stopped listening to what my teacher was lecturing on and was paying full attention to what was going on outside. Then the bell rang, and I bolted out of class. In the hall, there was a trail of blood, and I put two and two together. Something bad had happened.

It wasn't long until the news started making its way among the students that two girls had gotten in a fight, and one ended up in the hospital. Fights were pretty common at my school. But this time it went beyond what we normally experienced. These two girls, who really had nothing against each other, decided to fight each other because of a bunch of rumors flying around about them. Someone had started talking about how one girl hated the other, and even though it wasn't true, because of the rumors, the two girls felt like they had to fight it out to prove their positions. Only this time, during the fight, one girl pulled out a glass bottle and hit the other over the head. The glass shattered and slit her head wide open, which is what led to the trail of blood in the hall.

Luckily neither girl suffered any severe injuries. But the whole fight itself was pointless. Two people were at each other's throats, getting hurt, all because of a few rumors. That was just the environment I grew up in. Instead of talking through issues or finding a way to solve things without fighting, we were all growing up with the expectation that fighting was the way to solve problems. That violence was expected.

It wasn't just other people who fell into the trap of these expectations. I found myself caught up in it too. Most of the time, I was a pretty good kid. I studied hard, did what my mom told me to, and stayed out of trouble. But I had friends who thought it was cool to do things like vandalize someone else's property or steal something just to prove they could do it. They weren't hardened criminals. It was just the thing people in our neighborhood did, maybe out of boredom, maybe for the thrill, and definitely for the recognition they got from the other guys.

I had seen so many of my friends praised for stealing things, given admiration for getting by with something that was against the law, that I decided I wanted to do it too. After all, how hard could it be to steal something? And it seemed like the guys I knew never suffered any consequences.

IT CAN BE HUMAN NATURE FOR US TO LIVE OUT OTHER PEOPLE'S EXPECTATIONS OF US.

It can be human nature for us to live out other people's expectations of us. Those expectations—and the messages we receive about what we should be or could be—can be good or bad. We are all influenced by our environments. Whether it's the girls at my school fighting rather than talking things out or me altering my natural behavior to prove I was as cool as my friends, we were doing things with our lives that were expected of the kids in my neighborhood.

That instinct in us to live up to, or down to as the case may be, other people's expectations for us has actually been studied scientifically. Research done in the late 1960s by Robert Rosenthal and Lenore Jacobson showed that if teachers were led to expect enhanced performance from children, then the children's performance was enhanced (Rosenthal and Babad 1985). They gave an intelligence test to an entire class of children. Then the researchers told the teachers which students showed "unusual potential for growth." They labeled 20 percent of the students with that designation. But in reality, that group was picked at random. At the end of the year when the students were evaluated again, those 20 percent scored significantly higher.

The Pygmalion effect has been proven countless times over the years with research performed in areas other than education. Scientists have documented evidence of people working to meet others' expectations in family homes, courtrooms, military training centers, and business environments. In the initial Rosenthal and Jacobson study, the teachers gave the students positive messages and positive reinforcement, and many later studies looked at positive reinforcement as well. But I know, from my own childhood experiences, that we have a tendency to live our lives based on other people's expectations of us, whether those expectations are good or bad.

My neighborhood was one filled with low expectations that often resulted in higher violence and crime than other environments. It was just expected that most boys who lived there would grow up to be deadbeat dads or criminals because that's what usually happened. But growing up in a world surrounded by negative messages, I also had some positive reinforcement coming my way. My grandmother was one who really helped build my confidence. She was always telling me to look beyond my surroundings or that I was gifted at things.

I also give credit to my teachers as well for believing in me and helping me understand I could do something with my life. They would pull me to the side and say, "Be careful who you are hanging out with. You're better than that." Or they would let me know about things like the SAT and help me get signed up and take the tests. They helped me get on the right track to apply for college and let me know that I was college material.

We are all living our lives being told what we should do by others, whether it's friends, family, or even the media. There are expectations put on you by your parents, by society, and by your friends. Some of those messages and expectations you're given are negative, and some are positive. And what's even trickier is some might sound positive but be negative for you. What if someone tells you all your life, "You're smart; you should be a doctor." But inside you really don't want to be a doctor; you want to use your creativity and be an artist. That's a positive-sounding message that might have negative effects.

No matter how influential other people's expectations are and how strong the Pygmalion effect might be, you have the power to shape your own life. Only you can know what you really think and feel on the inside and how you want to portray that to the world through your personality and your career.

Over the past five decades, scores of scientists inspired by Rosenthal have tracked Pygmalion effects outside of educational settings. They've documented evidence of it in family homes, courtrooms, military training centers, and businesses—anywhere inspired leadership can make a difference. According to these reports, when managers have high hopes for their employees, the workers become more productive. When military instructors believe trainees have superior skills, the trainees perform better. Furthermore, when college men converse by telephone with women they've been told are attractive, they believe the women behave in more attractive ways.

Low expectations may be just as influential. Scientists have chronicled the impact of negative expectations in settings where they occur naturally, such as classrooms that "track" students from early youth and in society's treatment of stigmatized groups such as racial minorities, the poor, the elderly, the homeless, convicts, and children with learning disabilities.

The important thing is to understand the power of the Pygmalion effect and to be able to filter out the messages and expectations that bombard you on a daily basis. Listen to the people in your life who support you, and find encouragement from them. But don't let the negative messages shape your life. In the end, all it will do is make you live your life for someone else.

The goal of this book is to help you learn to understand who you are and who you want to be, and then to give you the tools to help you get there. Understanding the power of the Pygmalion effect is one tool to help you reach your end goal. When you understand the power of the messages flooding you on a daily basis, only then can you begin to filter it out, to let go of the negative and embrace the positive. Surround yourself with people who are positive influences and stay away from those who bring you down. After figuring out who you are and how to love yourself, this step in understanding the Pygmalion effect can take you even further in your journey of becoming the person you want to be.

put yourself in charge

Be sure that your goals are a result of your expectations for your life. Other people can advise and support you, but it's your actions that need to change to see the results you want.

choose carefully

Which area or expectation should you choose? You may want to consider concentrating on the area that will have the greatest impact on your happiness, health, and fulfillment.

make mental and physical notes

Having written down your ultimate goals, you should have a physical reminder—a notebook, Post-it notes, or the notes app in your phone—of what you're aiming for. Now take it a step further and make mental notes associating your behavior with the other outcomes in your life.

WHAT ARE YOUR TOP THREE EXPECTATIONS FOR YOURSELF?

1   2   3

THIS YEAR:

THIS MONTH:

THIS WEEK:

TODAY:

READING MORE MAY ENHANCE RELATIONSHIPS OR CHANGE YOUR THOUGHTS ON YOUR ROLE IN THIS WORLD.

Read More:
The Purpose
of Perspective

Many successful people never stop learning. There's a reason why the Department of Education conducted a study that revealed 70 percent of adults in professional or managerial roles continue their educations (2007). Reading can be one of the best ways to keep up with emerging trends, learn from experts, and get the ideas flowing. This is why many people see the value in their lives from resolving every year to read more. One of the reasons reading is popular on the New Year's Resolutions list is because reading is essential to success—success in school and in career development. For those who read regularly, it's no surprise that books are excellent ways to expand their knowledge on a variety of topics and shape and expand their perspectives.

For some, however, consistent reading is a challenge. In the past, it was a struggle for me to commit to reading because I felt distracted and often lazy. When I'd sit down on the couch with a seemingly fascinating book, I'd somehow remember that I needed to wash the car, or there were a few emails that I needed to return. It took a long time for me to realize that I loved reading—it's just that my own home was a distraction. So to accomplish my resolution to read more, I began setting aside specific time to leave the house and read somewhere with nothing to distract my attention.

Reading more added so many things to my life and helped to evolve my perspective about topics, history, culture, and individuals that I never would have been exposed to. The tough thing is, there's so much good content out there. I had to discover the type of books that interest me and where to find them. Once reading became a habit, it helped me to become a better writer with a more vivid imagination. Reading and exploring content outside of my normal topics of sports and business helped me to gain different perspectives on vital issues, whether they're of personal or professional interest.

BY READING MORE BOOKS, HOPEFULLY WE ALL WILL CONTINUE TO EVOLVE OUR PERSPECTIVES BY LEARNING MORE ABOUT THE PAST AS WELL AS CULTURES THAT MAY BE IN OUR CURRENT SURROUNDINGS.

By reading more books, hopefully we all will continue to evolve our perspectives by learning more about the past as well as cultures that may be in our current surroundings.

One early January morning when I was a teenager, I was sitting on a comfortable pew as I did most Sunday mornings. The church was half empty as a result of an ice storm in the preceding days. The pastor, a gifted communicator known for his nontraditional style of teaching and for challenging the perspective of his congregation, was speaking on the subject of time. Kairos and chronos were the two types of time he referred to. Chronos is quantitative and refers to clock time, time that can be measured—seconds, minutes, hours, years. We use it in words like chronological. Kairos on the other hand is qualitative. It measures moments, not minutes. Further, it refers to the *right* moment, the opportune moment, the perfect moment, the best time of your life. This double meaning of time would shape my perspective moving forward.

There is nothing in my life I love more than spending time with my daughter. It doesn't matter if it's helping out with homework, shooting baskets in the driveway, or just listening to music together the few minutes in the car as we drive to a friend's house. That's been true since the day she was born. I wanted to be with that beautiful little being as much as I possibly could, no matter what that meant for me. I would change her diaper, buckle her up in her car seat, and we'd go everywhere together.

One day I needed to get some things at the mall, so that's where Arden and I went. I was walking through the mall with her in the stroller, doing things I needed to do, like shopping for new shirts for work and picking up a pair of running shoes. As I paid for my purchases, keeping the stroller right next to me, the woman helping me said, "It's so great that you are out shopping with your daughter."

Of course, I can't go to the mall without stopping by the food court, so I grabbed an ice cream and shared it with Arden. A couple of women smiled as they saw me spooning ice cream into her mouth and remarked on what a great father I was. Over and over that day, people went out of their way to come up and tell me I was being a great dad. I soaked up all that admiration and was really feeling good about myself. But then I started to think, "Wait a minute—it's not like I'm doing anything great; I'm just at the mall with Arden." And once again, my perspective took on a new shape.

Why were people praising me for spending time with my daughter? Moms go shopping with their kids all the time. You hardly go to the supermarket without seeing a harried mother trying to figure out what to buy for that night's supper while pacifying a crying child in the buggy. Or take a trip to Target, and you'll see in almost every aisle a woman trying to get things she needs for her home while also talking to her kids about what they need or where they're going next.

I knew from a very young age that I wanted to be a good dad. The thing is, I didn't really have a great sense of what a dad should be. I had only seen the bad side of things. I remember a few times when I would come into the kitchen for breakfast and see my mom dressed up, and it wasn't even a Sunday. I'd ask her where she was going, and she'd tell me she was going back to court. She was not alone. The women in the neighborhood I grew up in spent a lot of time in court trying to get child support from fathers who disappeared when it came time to help raise their children. The expectation set for fathers in my neighborhood was pretty low. Very early on in my life, I got a sense of how society views men in the dynamic of the family, and it wasn't very impressive. Most of the time, dads weren't around for the day-to-day duties of raising kids, let alone available for a few visitations or regular with the child support. Not having my own father around left a lot of emptiness in me, and that was something I didn't want to happen to my own children.

For me, being an involved dad meant being around, being a part of my child's life, and showing her I was there for her no matter what. Why was that so important to me? Not only was it because I knew from my own experiences the hurt and sorrow that comes from growing up without a dad around, but also as I became an adult, I started observing in others just how important fathers are to helping people become successful. When I was in the Army, or later at work, I would be in places where people gave speeches or presentations, and so many of the times when they talked about how they became successful or how they got to where they were in life, they talked about their dads.

I paid attention to people who I knew were stable people emotionally, who were in a good places in their lives, and it seemed like they always talked about their dads being in involved in their lives. And on the other side of things, I saw kids I grew up with in my neighborhood who didn't have dads around who ended up doing drugs or even in jail. The outcomes were so different, and from what I could see, one key to success was having had a good father. So even before I was a father myself, that one thing I wanted to be in life was a good dad, one who was there for my child, who made a point to go to ball games and school activities, and who had a relationship with his kid.

What I realized that day at the mall was my focus up to that point was spending time with my daughter—you know chronos, the time that's measured. My focus was spending as much time with Arden to let her know how important she was to me. However, I learned a valuable lesson that day at the mall. The ladies handing out praises for having my daughter at the mall knew something that I didn't: what they saw was kairos—you know, special moments in time. Consciously, I was focused on debunking society's expectations for dads and the definition of time associated with it. But subconsciously, the time that I wanted to spend with Arden was more about making memories and creating moments in time versus the amount of time spent. I was experiencing what I like to call double vision. My vision of what I wanted to be as a dad and the time invested wasn't matching up with the women at the mall who knew the value of creating special moments with their dads. I had a clear vision of the type of dad I wanted to be, but I didn't understand the difference between investing time and spending time.

For me, I experienced double vision when it came to what I wanted to be as a father versus society's expectations of what a father should be. Society told me it was the norm for dads to ditch their kids on weekends and not follow through with child support—at least that's what I saw when I was a kid. And then even as I got older, society was telling me it was the mom's job to change the diapers, to feed the baby, and to organize playdates. I ran into families where the mom and dad were still married, but the dad would spend weekends at the golf course while the mom stayed with the kids. It just didn't match up—the vision I had for myself and the vision I felt like society had for me.

Double vision exists, and we find it in many facets of our lives, but we don't have to let society's view take over our own vision. The important thing is to put a stake in the ground and stick to it. Define

BE PREPARED TO CONSTANTLY EXPAND YOUR VISION AS YOU EXPAND YOUR PERSPECTIVE.

who you are and what you want to be, and go for it, no matter what roadblocks might come in your way. And be prepared to constantly expand your vision as you expand your perspective.

There were plenty of other ways I showed Arden my love for her over the years—ice cream at the mall is just one example. But the important takeaway is that there will be obstacles in your path on the way to achieving your goal; the key is to stick to your vision.

We know from the previous chapter and studying the Pygmalion effect just how influential other people's expectations and society's expectations can be. But I also know from my own personal experience that you can overcome the influence of the Pygmalion effect. When you start experiencing double vision yourself, remember that there are several ways to expand your perspective. My perspective was expanded that day at the mall. I had an idea of the type of father that I wanted to be. Constantly learning, reading, and challenging my perspective has allowed me to grow and understand how I can be even more impactful in my daughter's life. For you, reading more may enhance relationships or change your thoughts on your role in this world.

make it enjoyable

Find out what works for you. If you're more likely to go to a yoga class than run on the treadmill, write down the class times on your calendar.

learn from the past

Any time you fail to make a change, consider it a step toward your goal. Why? Because each sincere attempt represents a lesson learned.

give thanks for what you do

Forget perfection. Set your sights on finishing that marathon, not on running it. Sometimes completing the marathon walking is better than not completing it while running.

Today I'm grateful for these three things:

1 _____
  _____
  _____

2 _____
  _____
  _____

3 _____
  _____
  _____

And these three people:

_____

_____

_____

THE BEGINNING OF THE YEAR IS AN IDEAL TIME TO RECALIBRATE AND RECONNECT WITH FAMILY

Spend More Time with People Who Matter:
Quitting Is Not an Option

We are off to a new year or new season. And the new beginning is a great time to add spending time with people who matter, particularly family, to your list of resolutions. Spending time with people who matter seems like a pretty simple thing to do; however, between technology and busy schedules, many of us are missing out on chances to deepen relationships with the people whom we say matter most. The fact is, many of us claim to be a little busy or overwhelmed these days, and it's true. The beginning of the year is an ideal time to recalibrate and reconnect with family whom we haven't seen in a while, and the reward we will receive in return for prioritizing important people will be truly worth it.

Ideally, we'll make an effort to show these people that they are priorities by adding them into our schedules. If you think about it, we schedule many other things in our lives, so why not friends and family time? The things that matter, such as doctor visits, rounds of golf, and work commitments, are all on our schedule. Why isn't time with our families and friends on our calendars? Even with little things like practices, games, and other events going on in the evening, finding one or two nights a week when you can sit down for a phone call or as a family at the dinner table can make a difference. Connecting over a meal can give you time to talk—without any distractions. It helps us all to unplug and learn how to cook, and it might be the perfect time to talk about important things in their lives. As you are writing resolutions and prioritizing life, connecting with the people who matter most can be a great way to spend your year.

CONNECTING WITH THE PEOPLE WHO MATTER MOST CAN BE A GREAT WAY TO SPEND YOUR YEAR.

My first official, tax-paying job when I was sixteen was with the nation's largest fast-food chicken restaurant. I was pretty excited to earn a regular paycheck to support my growing desire for the newest kicks or the latest CD. The job was working after school and weekends with a flexible schedule that allowed me to hang out with friends and family. The job was off to a great start, but less than one month into the job, I had my first challenge as a working citizen.

It was a Friday night, and things were pretty busy. In our neighborhood, people were out doing things on Friday—going to the club, seeing a movie with friends, or just hanging out—and typically this was time that I would connect with my friends to hang out. But this time, I was working. Whether it was before, after, or during going out, eating was an important part of the plan. This was my first full day working without any training, and so far, the day was going as smoothly as I could have hoped. A few hours into my shift, I noticed people lining up in the lobby, and I was cooking chicken as fast as I could according to my step-by-step training, but it just wasn't fast enough. Eventually, waiting customers began to get impatient. The manager kept yelling back at me, "We need more crispy!" or "We need more legs!"

The thing was, my training had only consisted of cooking in a controlled environment. I hadn't had any training on time management and how to manage a large crowd. I hadn't put enough chicken in the fryer. I couldn't make what was in it cooker any faster. I was stuck, stressed out, and overwhelmed by my coworkers impatiently waiting for more chicken. Through the stress, I started to get mad.

I was mad at my manager for not giving me the heads up for this type of rush and not giving me the training to handle it. I was overwhelmed by my coworkers not understanding why the chicken was taking so much time. And I was mad at the people in line for just being there!

I got so fed up that night that I wanted to quit. But I couldn't!

I went home that night, calmed down a little bit, and started to try to figure out how to prepare, so the next time a big crowd came I would be ready. I figured out for myself that I needed to be aware of what was going on at the clubs and what new movies were coming out. If it was something big or really popular, there would be more people out, and I would need to be prepared with more chicken. I figured out how much of each type of chicken to cook based on what was popular in our neighborhood. And I asked for advice from my manager, knowing his experience would be a big help; he just didn't have much time to stop and help when we were busy because he was running a register or making up meals just like the rest of the team.

To add to my frustrations that night, I began to think about the fun my friends could be having without me. After all, this was one of our regular nights that we would pile into a car and head to our favorite skating rink. Roller-skating was one of our favorite pastimes. All of our neighborhood friends, the prettiest girls, and many of the best skaters in Detroit would go. Friday nights generally started with a stop at Coney Island to fill up on chili fries or a coney dog topped off with the best trash-talking centered around who was going to do what that night. The night generally ended with sweaty shirts and laughs on who fell in front of the pretty girls or who was left on the sidelines once a slow-skate song came on. But none of this was part of my new routine as a working-class citizen. The thought of quitting crossed my mind to eliminate the embarrassment of falling behind on the job coupled with the thought of my friends having the time of their lives without me.

The thought quickly faded as I realized that quitting was not an option! I couldn't think of an excuse creative enough that would allow my mom to agree with my decision. I definitely couldn't anticipate how my friends would react and would put me at the center of every joke if they found out that I quit because I was overwhelmed and embarrassed.

Instead, I figured that I had an opportunity to prove that I could solve this weekend rush dilemma. I could show a little resilience to bounce back from an overwhelming situation and figure out a way to make things better in the future. Webster's dictionary defines resilience as "the ability to become strong, healthy, or successful again after something bad happens." That's exactly what happened during those first few weeks at my new job. That night, with the crowd pressing in, was a pretty bad night. But instead of walking out on the job, I came back even stronger and more successful, finding ways to anticipate the crowd and be prepared.

One crazy night at a fast-food restaurant might not seem like a big roadblock. But it is just one example of what was a stressful time in my life. There have been plenty of others. Throughout my career I've faced times when I was overwhelmed with stress, when assignments were thrown at me, or my managers would give me goals that seemed unattainable. But every time life starts to look stressful or overwhelming, I just take a step back, look at the situation, and start to prioritize. Because quitting is not an option. I know my goal in life is to be a good father, to be successful at my career, and to be a leader in my community. I won't let a few speed bumps get in the way of my reaching those goals.

The thing is, no one likes to lose. And that's what it feels like when you're being thrown a curve ball or too many things start to stress you out. That one night at work when I was sixteen made me feel like a failure. I couldn't even get a handle on a job as easy as frying chicken! But I have realized that hitting a roadblock doesn't mean you've failed. You have to take a deep breath and figure out how to get around it and move on. Taking a step back from the situation doesn't mean admitting defeat; it just means you have to take some time to figure things out.

Just remember that the goal here isn't perfection. Instead, you should be working to do your best, taking steps to become the person you want to be, even if it means taking it slow or taking time to redouble your efforts. Quitting is not an option if you're going to make your goals.

Sometimes it might seem like quitting is the easiest way out of a situation. When things get tough, often our first instinct is just to walk away, to leave whatever is making us stressed out or overwhelmed. I have the opportunity to talk with many different groups of people, and one of those happened to be a group of kids at a basketball camp. This wasn't just any camp. It was an elite camp with some of the best players and coaches, designed to help guys get out in front of college coaches while they're still in high school to let the recruiters see what they're made of. Everyone at this camp plays their heart out, and the competition is tough. So what happens when they get elbowed and miss a layup or they're so exhausted from running sprints that they feel like they can't do another drill? Do they throw in the towel and give up out of frustration? The answer is no. They reach down deep inside and remember why they're there.

Basketball camp is just one example. In our travels down the road of life, we encounter many opportunities that help us reach our goals, as well as many roadblocks along the way. The way to make it past those roadblocks is to figure out what your goal is and commit to it. That gives you the power you need to navigate around the roadblocks.

But there are also a couple of tools I use to help overcome the roadblocks:

1. **Prioritize.** When you're in a situation where you're feeling overwhelmed or stressed out, it's important to remember you can't fix everything at once. Figure out what you need to do first in order to survive today. Then work on the other things one or two at a time.

2. **Maintain your willpower.** Even when you have a plan, it can be tough to stick with your commitment when other guys are pushing you around on the basketball court, or when the line for chicken is going out the door and you feel like everyone is yelling at you. That's when you have to dig deep within yourself. Just like you have the power within you to make a change in your life, you also have the power within you to stick with your goals and do what it takes to get there.

Remaining committed and prioritizing are the best ways to keep from giving up and quitting. I like to say, the objective isn't to hit a home run every time; you're just trying to get to first base. When you understand what you want to do and then make a commitment to it, you're not going to get there all at once. It's a process, a matter of steps. It's when we look at it all at once that we get overwhelmed and feel like quitting. Looking at it as the steps to take to get to the end goal helps keep us on track.

In your work to get to your end goal, understand that it's going to be difficult. It's not a matter of if something bad happens but when. But when you understand why you've made your commitment, it's a lot more difficult to quit when those roadblocks pop up.

invest your best daily

Whatever it is, go further and bounce back faster if you are continually investing in your "best self."

focus on progress, not perfection

Perfection is unattainable. Shoot for "pretty good." Don't beat yourself up with minor mishaps like you ate dessert because you were stressed or skipped the gym for a week because you were busy.

safeguard your environment

When your motivation is low, your environment becomes all the more powerful in terms of helping or hindering your healthy-living intentions.

List the five important people in your life who can help you to achieve your goals.

1 _____

2 _____

3 _____

4 _____

5 _____

ONCE YOU'VE KICKED FEAR OUT OF YOUR LIFE, YOU WILL BE FREE TO ENJOY THE MOMENT.

Face Fears and Insecurities:
Kick Fear This Year

Around the New Year, we see many people, including ourselves, making all types of resolutions about the things we want to accomplish over the next year. We see Post-it notes of things to do and motivational quotes showcased on refrigerators and computer monitors everywhere. We hear about how someone will lose weight or stop speaking negatively, another will propose, and finally someone will commit to saving more money.

Once the work begins and we're faced with the challenge of change, we can find ourselves in a place where we're constantly worrying and overcome with fear of the unknown. If we do this, come next year this time, we'll look back and think to ourselves, "Wow, that was a tough year, but we'll try again next year."

Fears could be anything. We've all got them. Fears and insecurities, while unpleasant and generally created by our own thoughts, prevent us from taking the first step to truly achieving the resolutions we previously committed to. Sometimes the thoughts are fleeting, disrupting our days and causing us to feel overwhelmed and inadequate. Negative thinking can also spiral out of control, so it's a good idea to have a few strategies in your back pocket to stop that insecurity train and accomplish those resolutions. So how can you manage these pesky negative thoughts and beliefs we call fear? Choosing to face one of them is something to be proud of. The true resolution that we need is the resolution to face fear and overcome it. The most important promise we can make to ourselves and those we love is not to give up, instead choosing to kick fear this year.

THE MOST IMPORTANT PROMISE WE CAN MAKE TO OURSELVES AND THOSE WE LOVE IS NOT TO GIVE UP, INSTEAD CHOOSING TO KICK FEAR THIS YEAR.

When I was in the tenth grade, I was given an assignment in English class to read Ralph Ellison's *The Invisible Man* and then write a synopsis of it. It was an awesome book. Even though it was set in the 1920s and '30s, I could identify with the struggles the narrator faced as he tried to find his way in the world. He faced violence and discrimination as a black man trying to make his way in a world where white people held the power. At the end, he realized the only way to live was to be true to himself. It really hit home with me, especially as a teenager trying to find my own place in the world.

I came to class the day the assignment was due and turned in my synopsis, proud of my work. But then my teacher, Mrs. Brooks, a firm yet understanding teacher, started calling on people to give their thoughts on the book. "Wait a minute," I thought, "We were just supposed to write a summary. She never said to prepare for discussion." As much as I loved *The Invisible Man*, the thought of talking in front of the class petrified me. As soon as she started calling on people, a million thoughts started running through my head. "What if she calls on me, and I say something wrong? What if everyone laughs at me? What if I stumble over my words? What if I don't even know the answer to the question she's asking me?"

I was so worried about what might happen if she called on me that I wasn't even paying attention to the discussion in the classroom. And the longer she went on asking questions, the more scared I became. I was having that conversation in my head, with all the what ifs, and wasn't paying attention to what was going on in the class around me. My mouth started getting dry, my hands were sweaty, and I kept running through those questions in my head, the what ifs.

Finally, after what seemed like hours but was only about 45 minutes, the bell rang. I felt a huge release as I bolted out of class, relieved that I made it through without being called on.

In that moment, during that class, fear had paralyzed me. Not only was I too scared to take part in a discussion of a book that I had read and loved, but also I was so busy focusing on my fears that I didn't even listen to what the others were saying.

That's what fear does. It paralyzes us; it keeps us from taking action. And in the end, it keeps us from participating in life and becoming who we want to be.

It wasn't just that one day in class where I let fear get the best of me. In a larger context, as a teenager, I was letting fear rule my life. I was constantly living in fear of being different, of standing out from the crowd, of having people mock me. I was trying to be what I thought people expected me, as a young black man, to be. But it wasn't who I really was inside. The fear of being different held me back from letting my own unique personality shine through.

That fear continued to hold me back even as an adult. There were times when I was in the Army when I might be up for a promotion, but I'd hold back and not go for it. What if I fail the test? What if I don't have what it takes for that position? What if it turns out I'm not a good leader? Because I was afraid to fail, because I had those what ifs running through my mind, I didn't go for it and passed up things that would have been great opportunities.

We all have fears in our lives. One of my biggest was a fear of failure and not living up to my fullest potential. I cared about what other people expected out of me and what other people thought of me. Because of that, I was constantly striving for perfection in the things I worked for and in turn constantly faced a fear of failure and letting other people down. All of those what ifs, whether it was what if I don't have the answer right in high school or what if I can't pass the training course in the Army, were a part of a fear of failure.

There are plenty of other fears that hold us back as well. You might have a fear of change, a fear of being different from others and made fun of, or a fear of disappointing your friends or family. Whatever you're afraid of, it's only hurting you if you let that fear hold you back and keep you from being the person you really want to be.

We all have fears, but this is the year to kick those fears

out of the way. Quit letting them be roadblocks in your life. You can even take those fears and anxieties and turn them into positive forces to help you move toward what it is you want to be and succeed in your goals.

WHATEVER YOU'RE AFRAID OF, IT'S ONLY HURTING YOU IF YOU LET THAT FEAR HOLD YOU BACK AND KEEP YOU FROM BEING THE PERSON YOU REALLY WANT TO BE.

The what ifs still go through my head today. It's the same conversation I'm having with myself in my head, only this time it's focused on different things. I find myself thinking, what if I don't fulfill my purpose in life? What if I can't impact people the way I want to and help others change their lives for the better? Only now, instead of paralyzing me and keeping me from taking action, those what ifs motivate me. I want to make sure I fulfill my purpose in life. I want to make sure I become the person I have dreamed of being: an impactful leader at work, in the community, and at church; someone people look up to and respect; someone about whom, at the end of the day, people can say, "He has really made a difference in the life of many." Those what ifs that go through my head help me realize that I'm working toward my goals, and I can't let fear of failing keep me from being the person I want to be.

The only way to turn that fear into a motivator to keep moving forward is to let go of the anxieties of the past. One thing I had to do was reconcile the fact that I wasn't going to be perfect at everything all the time. Sometimes you do fail, and that's OK. You learn from it and move on. Once I stopped striving for perfection, I was able to let go of a lot of anxiety.

Letting go of the past is the first step. Worrying about things that have already happened won't get you anywhere. Reliving events and situations in your head over and over creates a roadblock that keeps you from moving forward.

SOMETIMES YOU DO FAIL, AND THAT'S OK. YOU LEARN FROM IT AND MOVE ON.

The other part of the equation is to stop worrying about the future. Right here, today, we can't do anything about tomorrow. We don't have the ability to travel through time and see what will happen next year, next week, or even the next day.

The key is to live for today. Once you've kicked fear out of your life, you will be free to enjoy the moment. Let's live every day enjoying the day for what it is, not waking up thinking about yesterday and living with those regrets, or worrying about tomorrow. Instead, focus on today and where you're going in your life. Focus on who you want to be. Be present. Be in the moment. Enjoy being with your family or your friends. Enjoy the feel of the warm sunshine or the coolness of a light rain.

Once you let go of the fear and all the space it is taking up in your brain, along with the conversations going through your head and the feelings of anxiety, you will find you have so much more time and space to concentrate on the present. We're all more able to enjoy where we are and who we are once we make that decision to kick our fears out of the way and move forward. It's an exhilarating experience and one that is necessary to move forward with becoming the person you want to be.

The reality is, we don't have to leave our fears and insecurities because they don't really exist. We create them unconsciously. If we don't create them, they don't really exist. So, our question is essentially about how we change the thought process to stop creating them.

choose your own destination

Make sure your goal is something that will benefit your life and not just impress your friends or family.

consider other areas of impact

Think about other areas of your life that overcoming your fear will impact. Often, one improvement can have unforeseen improvements.

take breaks regularly

Change can be taxing both mentally and emotionally. Be sure to take breaks to be sure you finish the "race."

WHAT DOES YOUR MAP FOR OVERCOMING FEAR LOOK LIKE?

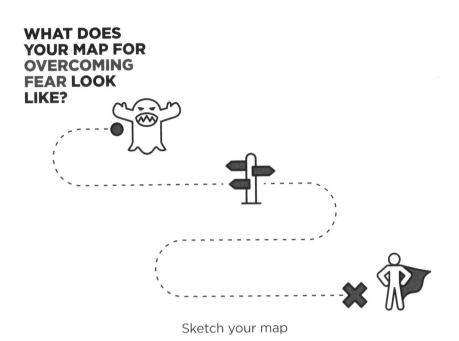

Sketch your map

THE **KEY** TO **ENJOYING LIFE** TO THE **FULLEST** LIES **NOT** IN **MAKING MAJOR** LIFE **CHANGES,** BUT IN **ACTIVELY PRACTICING ENJOYMENT** OF **LIFE** AS IT **CURRENTLY** IS.

CHAPTER

Enjoy Life to the Fullest:
Just Jump

Many Americans will use the new year or new season of life to reflect on past months or years and take stock of their lives. For many of us, a new year symbolizes a fresh start, kind of a chance to take up new hobbies, eliminate some bad habits, or reexamine life's priorities. In late 2015, GoBankingRates.com surveyed more than 5,000 people about their upcoming New Year's resolutions. When given the choice to make extreme money changes or add more fun to their lives, a larger percentage of people chose the latter. The survey found that the most popular resolution is, "Enjoy life to the fullest," with more than 45 percent of respondents opting for this choice (Kirkham 2015). The leading psychologist conducting the survey, Jonathan Fader, PhD, advises that the key to enjoying life to the fullest lies not in making major life changes, but in actively practicing enjoyment of life as it currently is. In an undated post on his blog he wrote, "Have

a daily ritual around enjoyment: Upon waking, ask yourself, 'What do I look forward to most today?.' At the end of your day, ask yourself, 'What was the most enjoyable part of my day and why?'"

Enjoying life sounds like a pleasant and beneficial resolution, but the failure rate is very high. The reality is, many of us work way too hard, and even if we are on vacation and don't work, we at least think of it. But there are several ways to successfully achieve the resolution.

Get creative and pay attention when others you know take excursions around your area. You can easily take day trips to check out nearby towns, hikes, lakes, a resort pool, nature reserve or park, or simply an obscure museum. Sometimes getting in the car and driving until you find something cool can be an adventure in and of itself. The point is to be intentional and ditch the excuses to enjoy life; just jump and make a decision to have fun regardless of the magnitude of the event.

BE INTENTIONAL AND DITCH THE EXCUSES TO ENJOY LIFE.

I remember standing on the edge of a twenty-foot platform, my toes curled around the edge. I was paralyzed in fear. Looking down, the water seemed much farther than twenty feet away. It looked like if I dropped, I'd be free-falling for ages. I looked up and saw the blue sky and sunshine, and it calmed me for just a minute. I had finally gotten the courage to climb up there, to attempt a jump off the twenty-foot platform, but once I got to the top I was afraid.

Looking down at the water again, a new wave of fear rushed over me. I was petrified. I had jumped off the ten-foot platform and thought I could do more. I had bravely climbed up the ladder and walked out to the edge. But once I was up there, twenty feet looked so much higher. I was so far up that it was quiet around me. I couldn't even hear the noise of the pool below, and the other kids looked like tiny doll people. My stomach gripped tight in fear. My knees started to tremble a little. It felt like I'd been up on that platform for an eternity trying to get up the nerve to jump. It was probably only a minute or two at the most, but the longer I waited, the more scared I got. And then I started having the conversation in my head; the *what ifs* started building up. "What if it hurts when I hit the water? What if something happens to me? What if water rushes up my nose, and I can't breathe?"

I was having this conversation in my head, and a kid behind me yelled, "Come on, man. Just jump." That was the trigger I needed. I counted down, "three, two, one," and jumped off. I closed my eyes, held my breath, and went for it. Those couple of seconds of free-falling out of the sky were exhilarating. I could feel the wind rushing up against me and felt my stomach jump up in my body, and then I splashed into the water, triumphant. I had done it. I faced my fear, climbed up that ladder, and jumped off the twenty-foot platform.

We've all had those moments in our lives where we've made it to the top of the ladder on the twenty-foot platform, but our fear paralyzed us, keeping us from making the jump, holding us back from taking the next steps toward our goals.

The diving platform is just an example. Fear can hold us back from doing many things, like asking a girl we've had a crush on out for a date, taking a promotion at work because we're afraid it will be too hard or take too much time, or attending college even after we've applied and been accepted because we're afraid to leave home or afraid we won't be able to handle the work load. As we work toward our goals in life, there are always instances where we'll face the unknown and have to wade in to unchartered territory to get to our goals. But then those anxieties and fears that fill our brains end up paralyzing us, keeping us from making the next step.

So how do you do it? How do you kick that fear aside and just make the jump forward?

The first step is to acknowledge your fear. Figure out what it is you are afraid of and what's driving that fear. For me, I used to be terrified to speak in public. Even though I knew I was prepared and had a good presentation, I was afraid I would stumble over my words, not get my point across, and just completely fail in front of everyone. I had to acknowledge that my real fear wasn't so much standing up and talking in front of people, but instead I was paralyzed by a fear of failure. That fear was what drove other fears in my life, like a fear of making presentations.

Once you acknowledge your fear, the next step is to embrace it. My fear of failure was affecting different parts of my life. I turned down promotions because I was afraid I wouldn't be able to do the work. I avoided getting involved in relationships with other people because I was afraid they might end up not liking who I was once they got to know me. But once I acknowledged that it was a fear of failure holding me back, I embraced that fear and worked to understand it. I was able to see that most of the things I have learned in my life came from times when I tried something and did fail. Failing at something, or not succeeding, doesn't mean it's the end. After all, if I did go out and stumble over some words in a presentation, I learned that it didn't cost me my job, my health, or my reputation. In fact, it might have even helped me in all of those areas, giving me a greater sense of confidence for next time knowing I could mess up a little and still do fine, and helping me realize that the important thing was getting my point across, not being a perfect presenter.

In fact, I learned that it was striving for perfection that held me back in many instances. I had an inner need to be perfect in anything I did, which meant I was constantly living with a fear of failing. Because really, who can be perfect at everything all the time? No one can, and I knew that. So instead of trying something and possibly failing, I would avoid things that I wasn't sure I could master with perfection.

In the end, I learned that perfectionism isn't the goal. The goal is to make progress. But you can't make any progress if you're not moving forward. When you're paralyzed by fear, you can't take that jump and move forward.

So after acknowledging your fear and embracing it, the next step is to channel that energy in a positive manner. Turn the negative thoughts that drive fear into positive thoughts that motivate you.

TURN THE NEGATIVE THOUGHTS THAT DRIVE FEAR INTO POSITIVE THOUGHTS THAT MOTIVATE YOU.

I still get anxious every time I talk in front of a group of people. But now instead of worrying about what will happen if something goes wrong, I turn that anxiety into positive energy to help me move forward. Before I give a talk, I give myself a pep talk. I'll tell myself that it's good there's such a large crowd in the audience because it gives me the opportunity to touch that many more people. I think about all the people I will be helping by sharing the information I've learned.

It's all about telling yourself a different story. It's about changing those conversations in your head from ones that stoke the anxiety and make it grow to ones that channel that emotion into something positive.

For example, if you've applied and been accepted to college but haven't decided to accept because you're afraid you won't be good enough, change the story you're telling yourself. Instead of worrying you won't succeed, think about the fact that the college wouldn't have accepted you if they didn't think you were able to do the work.

If you've had a crush on a girl for weeks but have been afraid to ask her out, change the story you tell yourself. Instead of worrying about whether she'll stay no, plan on her saying yes. Think about where you'll go out to eat and what you'll do. Imagine making her laugh and how much fun you'll have once you're together.

Another key to finding courage is to have a plan. Not only do you need to change the story you tell yourself in your head, but also you need to have a clear map of where you're going and how you're going to get there. I talk with a lot of people who seem to have a clear idea of what they want in life. They might say they want to go to college, or they want to be a professional athlete. But then my follow-up question is, "What are you doing to get there?" It's great to have a dream, but you have to have an action plan to get you moving toward that goal. Maybe the plan includes taking the right classes in high school, registering and studying for the ACT exam, and researching the colleges you want to apply to. All of those things are part of getting you to your goal of going to college.

The ability to "just jump" means taking a step forward, but it's hard to take a step forward if you don't have a plan for where you're going. Making the plan and having a clear path toward your goal is one way to find the courage to take that step forward. It can help you move, rather than leaving you paralyzed by fear.

Acknowledge your fear. Embrace your fear. Change the story you tell yourself. Make a plan. Then you'll have the courage to jump. Whether you're leaping off a twenty-foot platform, taking a new job, moving to a new city, or marrying the love of your life—or even if you're making a smaller jump like a promotion within your company, new classes in college, or a night out with new friends—it takes courage to move forward. But by following a few simple steps and by changing your mental game, you will have the confidence to take the next step.

Every plan faces roadblocks, and sometimes those roadblocks are our own fears. By facing those fears and finding the courage to just jump, you'll be able to move forward and get on your way to meeting your goals and becoming the person you want to be.

don't beat yourself up

Obsessing over the occasional slip won't help you achieve your goal. Do the best you can each day and take one day at a time.

congratulate yourself

Plan a reward! Write it down on your calendar, so you can keep your eyes on the prize!

go for it

If your resolution doesn't surprise you, keep writing.

Face Fears
Personal Contract

I, _____, vow to turn my fears and negative

thoughts into motivation.

My two to three biggest fears are:

1 _____

2 _____

3 _____

(Now scratch them out! They don't own you!)

This is how I will turn them into motivation:

_____

_____

_____

_____

Example: *I am afraid of public speaking.*

I get nervous energy before speaking to a crowd. I will
give that energy to my audience with an animated and
engaging presentation.

Closing Words

Perspective: When something bad happens, you can laugh it off, let out a sly smirk, or stay stark and sad—how you respond shapes your reality. And your response is entirely your choice.

Faith: Anxiety is often paralyzing. Stressing over things you can't control depletes your energy, shortens your life, and keeps you from sleeping. Faith in a higher power can free you.

Resilience: Every once in a while, life deals multiple setbacks. How quickly you dust yourself off, regroup, and keep moving dictates how quickly you get back on track.

Gratitude: In a world of likes, swipes, and follows, it's easy to get caught up in what you don't have. Give thanks instead for what you do have. Your thoughts determine the energy around you. Are you grumpy or grateful?

Courage: Once in a while, ask yourself, "What's the worst that could happen?" Fear prohibits you from truly living a perfectly imperfect and fulfilled life. Don't let "what ifs" hold you back.

Celebrate: Confetti, balloons, ice cream sundaes or a walk in the park—whatever your preferred celebratory method, remember to celebrate small wins as well as major victories.

Resources

Callaham, John. 2018. "The History of Android OS: Its Name, Origin and More." Android Authority. Accessed May 21, 2018. https://www.androidauthority.com/history-android-os-name-789433/.

Chan, Melissa. 2016. "LeBron James Speech at ESPY Awards: Read the Transcript." Time. Accessed May, 21 2018. http://time.com/4406289/lebron-james-carmelo-anthony-espy-awards-transcript/.

Duhigg, Charles. 2012. *The Power of Habit: Why We Do What We Do.* New York: Random House.

Ellison, Ralph. 1995. *Invisible Man.* New York: Vintage International.

Fader, Jonathan. n.d. "Three Ways to Enjoy Your Life More." Accessed May 21, 2018. https://jonathanfader.com/ways-enjoy-life/.

Goodreads. n.d. "A Quote by Anthon St. Maarten." Accessed May 21, 2018. https://www.goodreads.com/quotes/821092-dare-to-dream-if-you-did-not-have-the-capability.

Kirkham, Elyssa. 2015. "'Enjoying Life to the Fullest' Is 2016's Top New Year's Resolution, Survey Finds." GoBankingRates. Accessed May 21, 2018. https://www.gobankingrates.com/saving-money/budgeting/enjoying-life-2016s-top-new-years-resolution-survey/.

Leslie, Ian. 2015. *Curious: The Desire to Know and Why Your Future Depends on It.* New York, NY: Basic.

Oxford Dictionary, s.v. "FOMO (n.)." Accessed May 21, 2018. https://en.oxforddictionaries.com/definition/us/fomo.

Rosenthal, Robert, and **Elisha Y. Babad**. 1985. "Pygmalion in the Gymnasium." Educational Leadership (September 1985): 36-39. http://www.ascd.org/ASCD/pdf/journals/ed_lead/el_198509_rosenthal.pdf.

Turkle, Sherry. 2011. *Alone Together: Why We Expect More from Technology and Less from Each Other.* New York: Basic Books.

U.S. Department of Education, National Center for Education Statistics. 2007. "Fast Facts" excerpts from *The Condition of Education 2007.* Accessed May 21, 2018. https://nces.ed.gov/fastfacts/display.asp?id=89.

About the Author

REGINALD BEAN is vice president of culture, engagement, and stewardship for Coca-Cola Consolidated. In his role, Reginald is responsible for providing strategic direction and planning while promoting a purpose-driven, values-based culture through effective employee engagement. Additionally, Reginald's responsibilities include developing external relationships with strategic outreach organizations designed to enhance the experience for employees, customers, and partners.

Reginald began his career with Coca-Cola Consolidated in 1999 when he joined the company in territory sales. He held several positions within Coca Cola including director of multicultural marketing, director of finance-operations, director of sales analytics, and strategic planning analyst. Prior to joining Coca-Cola Consolidated, Reginald served his country in the US Army for seven years where he participated in several international desert and urban training missions.

Reginald holds an MBA with a concentration in leadership from the McColl School of Business at Queens University of Charlotte. Reginald enthusiastically serves the community holding board positions for the Blumenthal Performing Arts

Center, Wilberforce University, and Anuvia Prevention and Recovery Center. Reginald is a published author of the book *Unfinished: 40 Lessons on Purpose, Self, and Becoming a Man*, in which he inspires young men to discover themselves while positively impacting their families and communities. Reginald shares life's journey with his wife, Shavonda, and daughter, Arden. He enjoys numerous physical activities including riding his road bike and motorcycle.

CONNECT WITH REGINALD

reginaldbean.com

hello@reginaldbean.com

reginaldbean

reginaldbean

980.269.6261

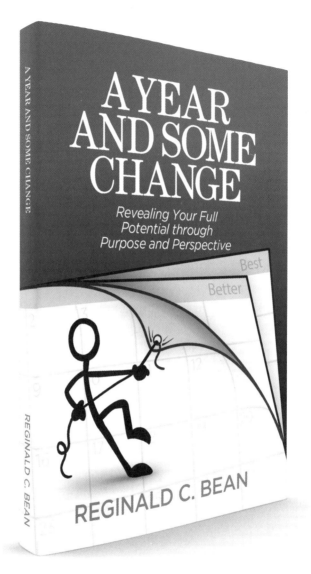

You've read each chapter, completed the exercises, and realized the areas of change necessary in your life ... now what? Share details of your progress at hello@reginaldbean.com or visit reginaldbean.com for additional resources.